5/05/01

TEACHING SHOP AND LABORATORY SUBJECTS

Albert J. Pautler
State University of
New York at Buffalo

Charles E. Merrill Publishing Company
A Bell & Howell Company
Columbus, Ohio

To: Marilyn, Mark, Ann, Mary Beth,
Michael, and My Parents.

THE MERRILL SERIES
IN CAREER PROGRAMS

International Standard Book Number: 0–675–09213–2

Library of Congress Catalog Card Number: 75–150076

1 2 3 4 5 6 7 8—76 75 74 73 72 71
Printed in the United States of America

THE MERRILL SERIES IN CAREER PROGRAMS

In recent years our nation has literally redis-covered education. Concurrently, many nations are considering educational programs in revolutionary terms. They now realize that education is the responsible link between social needs and social improvement. While traditionally Americans have been committed to the ideal of the optimal development of each individual, there is increased public appreciation and support of the values and benefits of education in general, and vocational and technical education in particular. With occupational education's demonstrated capacity to contribute to economic growth and national well being, it is only natural that it has been given increased prominence and importance in this educational climate.

With the increased recognition that the true resources of a nation are its human resources, occupational education programs are considered a form of investment in human capital—an investment which provides comparatively high returns to both the individual and society.

The Merrill Series in Career Programs is designed to provide a broad range of educational materials to assist members of the profession in providing effective and efficient programs of occupational education which contribute to an individual's becoming both a contributing economic producer and a responsible member of society.

iii

The series and its sub-series do not have a singular position or philosophy concerning the problems and alternatives in providing the broad range of offerings needed to prepare the nation's work force. Rather, authors are encouraged to develop and support independent positions and alternative strategies. A wide range of educational and occupational experiences and perspectives have been brought to bear through the Merrill Series in Career Programs National Editorial Board. These experiences, coupled with those of the authors, assure useful publications. I believe that this title, along with others in the series, will provide major assistance in further developing and extending viable educational programs to assist youth and adults in preparing for and furthering their careers.

Robert E. Taylor
Editorial Director
Series in Career Programs

FOREWORD

The beginning shop and laboratory teacher is faced with a multitude of problems. It is the purpose of this book to eliminate many of them through mastery of good teaching procedures and practices. Not only does the author provide the *how* to teaching in the shop or laboratory, but the *why* as well. To aid the teacher in keeping his perspective, the author stresses the point that schools and teaching exist for students.

As "manager" of the learning environment, the prospective or beginning teacher is taken step by step through a sequence of experiences which will lead to effective teaching. The reader will become caught up in the description of what is to be accomplished through pre-planning, beginning the school year, presenting the subject, and evaluating student-teacher progress. The interaction between student and teacher is emphasized.

Management of the learning environment is a key point throughout the publication. Good management results in good learning; whereas poor management breeds confusion. Tried and proven practices, successful procedures and suggested ideas to be further developed by the reader serve as the content of this publication.

The author, Albert Pautler, is a master teacher. His experience includes teaching at the secondary and university levels. As a "teacher of teachers," he knows the problems of those who aspire to impart skill and knowledge to others. This book is intended to assist in this process and is so written. What is left is for the reader to digest its content and apply its meaning to the teaching of shop and laboratory subjects. This, I am sure, would be Dr. Pautler's hope.

Carl J. Schaefer
Series Editor
Trade & Industrial Education

v

PREFACE

The focus of this book is on the beginning shop and laboratory teacher. The text should be of value to both pre-service and in-service vocational, technical, and industrial arts teachers and anyone responsible for teaching a shop or laboratory subject in the public schools, the military, or private industry.

Due to its particular format, the book would be most valuable when used as a text in a one semester course in methods and techniques of teaching shop and laboratory subjects. The first part of the book deals with the preparations a teacher should make before his classes actually begin. Such things as objectives of education, school policies and services, and shop organization and management are covered. An in depth study of lesson planning is made in the second part. The author not only discusses the organization of teaching materials; he also talks about what should be taught. The third part covers the presentation aspect of teaching, including: first day procedures, the teaching-learning situation, and aids and methods of instruction. The book closes with a section dealing with both the theoretical and practical sides of evaluation and grading. As an aid to teachers and students, each chapter is divided into three sections: (1) presentation of new material, (2) discussion questions, and (3) assignments.

The author would like to thank the many pre-service and in-service teachers with whom he had the opportunity to work in the Department of Vocational-Technical Education at Rutgers—The State University. Special thanks are extended to Dr. Carl Schaefer, Chairman of the Department, for his encouragement and advice in the preparation of this book. Use of the forms and records displayed in the book was made possible by Dr. Burr Coe, Superintendent, Middlesex County Vocational-Technical Schools, East Brunswick, New Jersey.

Albert J. Pautler

CONTENTS

Contents

Part I   PREPARATION

Chapter 1 THE NEW TEACHER AND HIS ASSIGNMENT

Every September teachers from a variety of backgrounds enter the field of education. These backgrounds can include college, employment in business and industry, and experiences in trade, industrial, or technical education specializations.

Most new teachers have had some teaching experience at some time during their lives. It may have been as a student teacher, intern teacher, or as an instructor in the military, church, civic related organizations, or night school.

This book will deal mainly with the person entering teaching with no formal teaching background. However, the material included should be useful to all teachers preparing to teach shop or laboratory subjects in junior high schools, middle schools, senior high schools, technical institutes, and community colleges.

This chapter deals with the basic objectives of general and occupational education and discusses the stated objectives of the typical local school. It offers the new teacher some educational philosophy which he may find useful.

Occupational Education and Its Objectives

The phrase, occupational education, refers to an educational program especially designed to prepare the learner for employment upon completion of the program. It includes all the areas associated with vocational education including industrial arts, technical education, trade and industrial education, and the health and service occupations. These areas can be further broken down. Industrial arts is the study of industry and the products, processes, and materials associated with it. Technical education programs include electronics, industrial chemistry, instrumentation, machine design, nuclear technology, and others. Trade and industrial education programs consist of automotive repair, carpentry, dressmaking and design, machine shop, plumbing, and others. The health occupations would include dental assistance, medical assistance, practical nursing, nurses aides, and others. Service trades programs are made up of food service, distributive occupations, building maintenance, service station sales, and others.

The primary objective of occupational education programs is the preparation of students for entry level employment. According to this objective, a teacher's final program evaluation should be based on the success or failure of the students to gain entry level employment within their specializations. The primary course objective should be the employability of the individual upon completion of your course as well as whatever other positive influence your association with the student will have on him.

This does not imply that the shop and laboratory teacher is concerned only with the employment of his students. A teacher should be concerned with the total student and not just the subject matter relationship which exists in all classroom situations. In other words, be concerned with the individual and your total relationship with him. As early as 1918, people realized this important idea of the student as an individual. At this time the Commission of the Reorganization of Secondary Education, which had been established in 1913 by the National Education Association, issued a statement entitled, *Cardinal Principles of Secondary Education*. The statement identified the following seven aims or principles of secondary education.

1. Sound health, knowledge and habits.
2. Command of the fundamental processes (reading, writing, arithmetical computation, and oral and written expression).
3. Worthy home membership.
4. Education for a vocation.
5. Education for good citizenship.

6. Worthy use of leisure.
7. Ethical character.[1]

These aims are still important today. When asked what he taught, one teacher always replied, "Students." His first responsibility was always to the total student and his secondary responsibility was to subject matter. The impact of the teacher-pupil relationship will be a much longer lasting one than the subject matter involved in the relationship. Likewise, always remember that schools exist for students and not for teachers, principals, and guidance counselors.

If it were not for students, the teachers and administrators would not be employed in the educational system. Many experienced teachers have soured to the point of feeling sorry for themselves and developing the attitude that they were doing the students a great favor by teaching. When a teacher feels this, he should get out of teaching before a negative influence is conveyed to his students.

The National Education Association Commission on Educational Policies identified the following *Ten Imperative Needs of Youth.*

1. All youth need to develop salable skills and those understandings and attitudes that make the worker an intelligent and productive participant in the economic life. To this end, most youth need supervised work experience as well as education in the skills and knowledge of their occupations.
2. All youth need to develop and maintain good health and physical fitness.
3. All youth need to understand the rights and duties of the citizen of a democratic society, and to be diligent and competent in the performance of their obligations as members of the community and citizens of the state and nation.
4. All youth need to understand the significance of the family for the individual and society and the conditions conducive to successful family life.
5. All youth need to know how to purchase and use goods and services intelligently, understanding both the values received by the consumer and the economic consequences of their acts.
6. All youth need to understand the methods of science, the influence of science on human life, and the main scientific facts concerning the nature of the world and of man.
7. All youth need opportunities to develop their capacities to appreciate beauty in literature, art, music, and nature.

---

[1]Commission of the Reorganization of Secondary Education, *Cardinal Principles of Secondary Education.* (Washington, D.C.: U.S. Office of Education, Bulletin 35, 1918), p. 10.

8. All youth need to be able to use their leisure time well and to budget it wisely, balancing activities that yield satisfactions to the individual with those that are socially useful.
9. All youth need to develop respect for other persons, to grow in their insight into ethical values and principles, and to be able to live and work cooperatively with others.
10. All youth need to grow in their ability to think rationally, to express their thoughts clearly, and to read and listen with understanding.[2]

If fulfilled, these needs would satisfy not only the objectives of vocational education but also the ultimate goal of most educational programs which is the development of a worthwhile citizen who can function in a democratic society.

The Stated Objectives of Your School

Most schools have some general statement of philosophy as well as stated objectives that guide their operation in providing quality education for the students. As a person looking for a first teaching position or as a new teacher, you might want to ask the principal about the school philosophy and stated objectives that influence the faculty, students and most important, the curriculum of the school. Unless you are employed as a teacher in a new school, you will have little control over the existing philosophy and objectives under which you will be required to work. However, it is to your advantage to be acquainted with the existing objectives. Later as a new philosophy or a new listing of objectives is developed, your voice will be heard. The stated philosophy and objectives should be developed by means of faculty, student, and community committees working together to provide the best and most meaningful program possible for the students. When a program is being evaluated, it should be done so in terms of the stated objectives. An agreement and a common effort should be made by all staff members to carry out the stated objectives.

The following list is an example of one school's stated functions of the high school curriculum:

1. To help every student grow up successfully in our society through meeting and carrying out his developmental tasks.

---

[2]Educational Policies Commission, *Education for All American Youth.* (Washington, D.C.: National Education Association, 1944), pp. 225-226.

2. To teach the essential understandings, habits, and attitudes necessary for good physical health.
3. To make available to each student a chance to sample a variety of recreational activities and interests and to develop skill in some of them.
4. To provide each student with vocational guidance and that part of occupational education needed for vocational effectiveness in the world of work.
5. To evaluate community provisions for health, recreation, housing, employment, etc., to call attention to needs and lacks in these areas, and to promote community action where needs and lacks exist.
6. To provide in all aspects of school life a living example of the first principle of democratic human relationships — respect for the dignity of the human individual.
7. To teach the skills of democratic group planning and discussion.
8. To teach the skills of reflective thinking and group problem solving.
9. To support the family as an institution by a realistic study of the problems and difficulties confronting the family today. To work with homes, churches, and other agencies on these problems.
10. To develop an understanding of world-wide social problems and a sense of responsible concern for our country's role in world affairs.
11. To develop a sense of responsibility and concern for the welfare of the local community.
12. To study continuously the meaning of democracy, to create awareness of needs for enrichment of that meaning, to protest against violations of the basic democratic faith.
13. To help students begin to formulate values and standards.
14. To help students continue developing needed proficiency in various skill areas—language skills, number skills, consumer skills, etc.

In chapter four, the concern will be with determining what to teach. The subject will then be the stated objectives of your particular course, be it automotive, cosmetology, practical nursing or any other specialization taught in a shop or laboratory environment. So a concern with the objectives that influence the total school are a valid consideration for the beginning teacher.

It is of course possible that your request to see the stated philosophy and objectives of the school might be met with a blank stare from the principal. It is possible, but not probable, that the school is operating without any clearly written statement of objectives. If, however, this is the case, your request might prompt a committee to develop such a statement. As stated earlier, a statement of this nature should come about as a result of faculty, student, and community involvement. All parties involved should be brought in early and actively engaged in the development of the philosophy and stated objectives.

The School Administration

As a new teacher, you will want to become well acquainted with your building administrator. In most cases, he will carry the title of principal. The principal can be invaluable in helping beginning teachers see their own roles and recognizing individual abilities. He can provide ways for teachers to see how they are a part of the total curriculum and engender a concern on the part of his staff members that extends beyond the scope of each special area and encompasses the broader interests of the school.

A principal is a human being and as such has both the inherent strengths and weaknesses. Because the principal is in a position of authority, he comes under much pressure from forces both within and without the school. Please remember this in your relationship with him. It is to your advantage to speak with him and some of his staff members before accepting a position within the school. You will have a great deal of contact with him after you are employed, so make sure that he is the kind of person with and for whom you will be able to work.

The principal assumes the responsibility for the quality of the total program in the school. It is, therefore, one of his most important functions to see that the program meets all of the standards required of a total curriculum. In the vocational setting, this means that the program is designed to meet the educational needs, both short and long term, of all the students enrolled. This, in turn, means that students of widely varying interests and abilities should be able to find satisfying and worthwhile educational experience within the framework of the subject offerings.

The principal may not be well versed in every subject area offered in his school; however, he is expected to see that the offerings do meet the needs of the students and the society in which they will ultimately find employment. This requires that he, as the educational leader of his school, know his students and the community from which they come, in addition to the community into which they will most likely go upon graduation. From these understandings should grow the educational objectives upon which the curriculum and its related learning experiences are based. The principal must see to it that the educational objectives of the program are stated in such a way that the outcomes may be objectively and accurately measured.

As teachers evaluate their own progress and come up with suggestions for improvement, the principal can be instrumental in making their innovations work by providing them with assistance in implementing their ideas. It is the principal's responsibility to create a suitable climate in the school to foster the best educational system possible. The teachers can help or hinder the principal to achieve this climate. The point is to learn as much about the school, the principal, and staff members as possible before signing a contract.

Fellow Staff Members

The relationship established with other staff members is as important as the relationship with the principal. Experienced teachers on the staff can be a very valuable source of information and assistance to the beginning teacher.

Some schools have the policy of assigning a new teacher to a more experienced teacher for the first year of his teaching career. The new teacher is then able to go to a fellow staff member for advice rather than have to go it alone. This system can work out rather well, provided that the experienced teacher is able and willing to spend time with the new teacher.

At times during the school year, you, no doubt, will be asked to serve on various committees within the school. These committee assignments will give you the opportunity to interact in a professional relationship with other teachers and administrators. Use caution in the extent to which social relationships develop with administrators. Let the administrator establish the rules and the name of the game. Some teachers have established social relationships which later resulted in school relationship problems. Look upon fellow staff members and yourself as members of a team which functions to provide the best educational program possible for the students.

The Students

As has been stated earlier, schools exist for students and not as employment locations for teachers. You are employed as a teacher because students desire an education and come to school for that reason.

Students can make or break a new teacher in a very short time. The total student population of the school will determine the atmosphere that exists in the school. How administrators and faculty treat and handle students will also affect the school's atmosphere.

As a teacher, you will have contact with students on a one-to-one basis, small group basis, and class size basis. Your relationship with students will largely determine your success or failure in the teaching profession. You will function as teacher, counselor, and personal advisor to students in your day-to-day activities.

Always remember the dignity of the individual, the student, in your relationship with him. He is a human being first, and your student second. Treat each student as you would like to be treated. Attempt to be firm, fair, and consistent in your relationship with students.

Personal Appearance

First impressions are important. When making your first contact in applying for your first teaching position, be properly dressed. Your first contact will probably be with the school principal. Present yourself to him just as you would appear before the students.

No matter what shop or laboratory subject you will teach, enter and leave the school just as if you were teaching English, history, or mathematics. Since you are a shop specialist, it does not mean that you come to work dressed any differently than the principal or related subjects teachers.

If a shop coat is necessary in your shop, keep it clean and in suitable condition. You are on daily display to your students and fellow faculty members. If you, as the teacher, wear dirty shop clothes, they will take the same privilege and follow your lead.

Many automotive mechanics and machine shop teachers look as if they have their shop coats cleaned yearly; others always appear to have a clean, well fitting shop coat. In most cases, the students reflect the same style as established by the teacher.

Maintain a suitable personal appearance and encourage the same from your students. They are preparing for the world of work as well as for life in general. Teach them good work habits as well as good personal habits. Remember your new role is as a teacher, not as a plumber, baker, or cosmetologist. You are employed as a teacher first, and as a subject matter specialist second.

DISCUSSION QUESTIONS

1. Develop a list of occupational education objectives that best fits the needs of your community, school, and students.

2. As a class project, request two or three first-year teachers to be guests in class. Ask them to discuss their reactions to their first year of teaching. After the formal presentations, break into two or three small groups, with a first-year teacher assigned to each group, and encourage open discussions.

3. As a class project, request a local vocational school principal to be a guest speaker in class. Assign him a topic dealing with typical problems of first-year teachers. Encourage an open class discussion after his formal remarks.

ASSIGNMENTS

1. Contact a local vocational school and ask for a copy of the school's stated philosophy. Comment in written form on the philosophy.

2. Obtain a statement of the objectives of a local vocational school. Comment in written form on the stated objectives.

3. Make a list of your strengths and weaknesses, as you view them, for your new position as a teacher. Be as objective as possible and use every technique possible to improve on your stated weaknesses. It will be the purpose of this course to help you improve to your maximum ability.

ADDITIONAL REFERENCES

American Vocational Association, *Trade and Industrial Education — The Challenge*. A statement of position of the Trade and Industrial Division, AVA. Washington, D.C.: American Vocational Association, 1962.

Bennett, Charles A., *History of Manual and Industrial Education 1870 to 1917*. Peoria: Charles A. Bennett Co., Inc., 1937.

Conant, James B., *The American High School Today*. New York: McGraw-Hill Book Company, 1959.

Conant, James B., *Slums and Suburbs*. New York: McGraw-Hill Book Company, 1961.

Conant, James B., *Thomas Jefferson and the Development of American Public Education*. Berkeley: University of California Press, 1962.

Dexter, Edwin Grant, *History of Education in the United States*. London: The Macmillan Company, 1914.

De Young, Chris A., *American Education*. New York: McGraw-Hill Book Company, 1960.

Gardner, John W., *Excellence: Can We Be Equal and Excellent Too?* New York: Harper & Row, Publishers, 1961.

Gardner, John W., *From High School to Job*. New York: Carnegie Corporation, 1960.

Hawkins, Prosser Wright, *Development of Vocational Education*. Chicago: American Technical Society, 1951.

Levitan, Sar A., *Vocational Education and Federal Policy*. Kalamazoo: W. E. Upjohn Institute, 1963.

National Manpower Council, *Education and Manpower*. New York: Columbia University Press, 1960.

National Manpower Council, *A Policy for Skilled Manpower*. New York: Columbia University Press, 1954.

Office of Education, *Vocational Education in the Next Decade: Proposals for Discussion*. Washington, D.C.: U. S. Department of Health, Education and Welfare, 1961.

Panel of Consultants on Vocational Education, *Education for a Changing World of Work*. A report to the President. Washington, D.C.: U.S. Department of Health, Education and Welfare (OE 80021), 1963.

President's Commission on National Goals, *Goals for Americans*. Englewood Cliffs: Prentice-Hall, Inc., 1960.

Prospectus of the Manual Training School of Washington University. St. Louis: Washington University, 1879.

Prosser, Charles A. and Charles R. Allen, *Vocational Education in a Democracy*. New York: Century House, Inc., 1925.

Research Council of the Great Cities Program for School Improvement, *Education for Tomorrow's World of Work*. Special Report for the Panel Consultants on Vocational Education. Chicago: Research Council of the Great Cities Program for School Improvement, 1962.

Rose, Homer C., *The Instructor and His Job*. Chicago: American Technical Society, 1966.

Swanson, J. Chester, *Development of Federal Legislation for Vocational Education*. Chicago: American Technical Society, 1962.

Venn, Grant, *Man, Education and Work*. Washington, D.C.: American Council on Education, 1964.

Chapter 2 BEGINNING THE SCHOOL YEAR

After you have agreed on teaching terms by means of a salary agreement or contract with your school district, some intermediate steps can be taken before the first day of school.

After Your Contract Is Signed

At this point, you should be familiar with the objectives of education and the specific objectives of occupational education and those of your school. You should also be somewhat familiar with the administrators and fellow staff members of your school. Your decision to teach in a certain school was your decision, and no one forced you to take this position. Do not agree to terms if you are doing so in order to get in and then fight to change a known bad situation. Your decision should have been a free one and not forced.

Regardless of whether you are entering teaching directly from industry without any student teaching or after a university program geared to teaching, you will still undergo a real transition period from your past role as worker or college student to that of teacher. Make good use of the time available to you before the first day of school. It may vary from a few days to a few months depending upon when you entered into a salary agreement with the school district. You will have to be the judge and use whatever time is available to you to the best possible advantage.

Professional Staff Guidelines

Most school districts will have some professional guidelines within which the staff is expected to function. You should give careful consideration to the material contained within these guidelines and become well acquainted with the rules and procedures which have been developed. Some of the items of concern follow.

1. Statement of Philosophy. This is usually in the form of a general statement of philosophy which has been written and approved by the board of education and should provide for the educational setting within the school district. It should provide for the total instructional staff as well as the individual teacher. Within it or from it should emerge the stated objectives that guide the total school program. It should reflect the feeling of the community, students and staff for the betterment of the all-school program.

2. General Policies. General policies will vary greatly from school district to school district. They might include such things as employment requirements, personal performance, association membership, community participation, and many other policies of a general nature.

3. Administrative and Staff Organization. Most professional guidelines will show a chart to illustrate the administrative and staff organizational system used within the school system. Small school systems will have a rather simple organizational chart, and larger districts will have rather complex charts. It is a good idea for new teachers to become familiar with the organizational chart and the chain of command system that exists. A full job description of each administrator and department chairman will usually be stated in the guidelines as well.

4. Position Descriptions. A description of each administrative position will be given in the guidelines. If the school system uses department chairmen and special personnel such as a director of guidance or a curriculum coordinator, a description of these positions will also be given in the guidelines. Some guidelines fail to list the shop and classroom teacher's job descriptions, but a good set of guidelines will include a statement concerning the teacher's role.

It should be helpful to the new teacher to review the job descriptions of all staff members. Doing so will give him an idea of the responsibilities placed upon each member of the staff. It will also be helpful in case of questions and to whom certain questions should be directed.

5. Salary Schedule. Salary guides or schedules are public record and no big secret. Each person in the community, as a tax payer, has a right to the salary schedule.

No doubt, one of the first things you will see in talking to administrators about a position will be the salary schedule. Study it well and be well versed about advancement and the maximum salary you can eventually obtain. Be especially concerned about added salary based on additional study and if the schedule is for a ten, eleven or twelve-month year.

6. Special Regulations. Any number of special state and local regulations might be included in this section of the guidelines. A number of items are worthy of consideration.

Most school districts offer some type of policy concerning absences and sick leave. Be concerned with the number of sick days and the maximum number that can be accumulated over a number of years. Some districts might offer the difference in your salary and that of a substitute to you, after all your normal sick days have been used up.

A statement concerning leaves of absence is usually included in the guidelines. This might cover maternity leaves and leaves for military training or other reasons.

Some districts might offer a sabbatical leave program. Sabbatical leaves are usually for the purpose of professional improvement which, in some cases, might include travel within the country or to foreign countries.

Sabbatical leaves, if offered by the district, usually require seven years of service, before one may qualify. They usually offer half pay for a full year or full pay for one semester. Sabbatical leaves are especially valuable in allowing someone a year to complete a masters or doctoral degree. Not all school districts have a sabbatical leave policy so be sure to check into the availability early in your teaching career.

You should also be concerned with the retirement benefits, annuities, professional liability insurance, health and life insurance, and medical insurance. Some districts will even pay your college tuition if you pursue an advanced degree which will benefit you as well as the district.

An attempt has been made to touch upon the major items contained in guidelines which would be of interest to a new teacher. A system or policy usually exists for student control and treatment. If such a policy exists, you should obtain a copy of it.

Pupil Personnel Services

A very important aspect of any school program is the department of Pupil Personnel Services (PPS). Larger school districts will have a department level structure for the PPS in the school, while smaller schools will use a different type of arrangement with perhaps just one guidance counselor performing the PPS function.

The guidance service is just one of a number of services that is included in PPS. Some of the other services may be: health services, financial assistance, psychological services, reading specialists, attendance services, social services, and others as they may be available within the school.

All teachers should be aware of what special services are available for the students. In most schools, a teacher can refer a student to his guidance counselor for special needs. The guidance counselor, through consultation with others, makes the final decision concerning the need for special services. However, the teacher is usually the one who will or should refer the student to such services. The teacher, and especially the shop teacher, has more contact with students than anyone else in the school. This is because most shop or laboratory courses are in session for two or three hours per day. Who should get to know students better than the shop instructor?

A brief review of some of the pupil personnel services seems appropriate at this point.

GUIDANCE SERVICE

Guidance services consist of a number of individual services such as student orientation, educational-vocational-personal guidance, educational and occupational information, reports to parents, job placement, and follow-up studies of graduates. Each student is assigned to a counselor. Each counselor may be assigned one hundred to three hundred students depending upon the school ratio of students to counselors.

With a ratio of one counselor to one hundred to three hundred students, it should be obvious that both students and counselors could stand some help. Therefore, each teacher in the school performs as an unofficial guidance counselor for his students. This is part of the job, and most teachers willingly perform the role. However, students with special problems should be referred to the guidance counselor. Counselors have special training and education to perform the best service possible for the students.

HEALTH SERVICES

Health services may include dental, physical, and psychological specializations. The services vary depending upon the size of the school and the availability of professional staff. Some schools may have a full-time school nurse in the building. She acts as a clearing house for referrals, accidents, and first aid cases. A school nurse is usually a nurse-teacher who can be asked to be a guest speaker in your class. She is concerned with body care as well as accident prevention. The school nurse can be a resource speaker in your class; ask her in sometime.

FINANCIAL ASSISTANCE

Someone in the PPS department may be assigned the responsibility of rendering financial advice to students. This advice might be in the form of a clearing house for part-time jobs that are available within the school and community or sources of financial aid for college. In smaller schools, the guidance counselor performs this role.

PSYCHOLOGICAL SERVICES

Counseling of a greater depth than that within the ability of a guidance counselor is sometimes required by students. Students who are troubled by a severe disturbance or persistent problem might need the service of a psychologist or psychiatrist. Many schools have full time psychologists, and others have part-time psychologists on the staff. Referrals to psychological services are usually through the guidance counselor in consultation with the building principal.

READING SPECIALISTS

Depending upon the type and size of the school, a reading specialist might be available. Poor reading ability is probably one of the major causes of academic difficulty in school. Reading specialists are individuals especially educated to help improve the reading ability of students. A teacher who feels a student has a reading problem should discuss the case with the student's guidance counselor who, in turn, can arrange remedial reading instruction if it is needed by the student.

ATTENDANCE SERVICES

If the school has someone assigned to attendance, that person would probably be in the PPS department. The attendance officer would be responsible for checking on students who are continually late or absent from school. He would maintain contact between the school and the home. He would attempt to rectify the problem and encourage promptness and better school attendance.

SOCIAL SERVICES

Along with mental hygiene and other pressures, social work has helped to show the influence of out-of-school groups, particularly the home, upon the student's in-school behavior. Teachers are learning that the pupil's school problems cannot be divorced from his home situation. Social services in the form of a visiting teacher or social case worker can provide another source of aid to the student and teaching staff.

The Classroom

Your shop or laboratory will be the place where you spend most of your time. It will be to your advantage to make the shop into the best possible teaching-learning situation. Being a new teacher, it will not be easy for you to evaluate the condition of the shop in which you will be teaching. This will be true whether the shop is in an old or a brand new school. You must teach in the shop before you can evaluate its effectiveness as a teaching-learning center.

If time permits and you are willing, some time spent in the shop or laboratory before school opens might be of great value. It would be nice if all teachers were given about a two-week head start on the students to get organized for a new school term. This is especially important for the new teacher, but unfortunately this is not common practice in school districts.

Student Evaluation

It is wise for the new teacher to look into the school policy for evaluation of students. The result of the evaluation is usually a grade which appears on the student's report card. The school will have some system of evaluation and some form of reporting procedure.

Some schools report grades every ten weeks. The grades are usually recorded on some form of report card which, in turn, is mailed or taken by the student to his parents. Many school systems use a data processing system of reporting grades, and this can be a time saving feature for the teachers. Since report cards and reporting systems differ from school to school, it would be difficult to do justice to all types. It is best for the new teacher to study the method in operation within his school system.

Grades are reported at various times during the year for the purpose of indicating the progress being made by the student. The report card is designed to acquaint the student and his parents with his progress in school. Some report cards have a space for the teachers to direct comments to the parents and parents to add comments as well. A parent may want to request a conference with the teacher and so notes this request on the returned report card.

Just as types of report cards vary, so do the methods of grading. Some schools use letter grades and others, numerical grades. A few basic systems are worthy of note.

1. A   Excellent
   B   Good
   C   Satisfactory
   D   Poor (lowest passing grade)
   F   Failing

2. A   90–100
   B   80–89
   C   70–79
   D   65–69
   F   Lower than 65

3. A   92–100
   B+   85–91
   B   80–84
   C+   75–79
   C   70–74
   D   65–69
   F   Lower than 65

In the first system, letter grades are reported on the report card. An *A* means excellent, and an *F* means failure. In the second system, either numerical grades or letter grades could be reported on the card. If the student's class average was 87 and the school reported by means of letter grades, his grade would be *B*. If the school reported in numerical grades, the 87 would appear on the card. The third system may be reported in either numerical or letter grades. The third system makes use of *B* + and *C* + grades, whereas the second system does not.

A great amount of time can be spent in faculty committees and faculty meetings deciding upon a grading system. No doubt, whatever system is used, it will have both strong and weak features and favorable and unfavorable reaction from faculty members.

Remember, faculty members place grades on cards, but the student and his or her parents must interpret the meaning. If a faculty is changing the report card or the grading system, it would be wise to include both students and parents on the committee that is charged with the task of developing a new card or grading system.

The new teacher should look at the grading system and report card used by the school district. Remember, it is the teacher who must make the decision on what grade to assign the student. Chapter fifteen will deal more directly with evaluation, grading, and statistics for the classroom teachers. Please remember that the teacher is an important decision maker in deciding on a system to use in the laboratory or shop for evaluating students. The grades the student *earns* will be reported on the report cards. The student earns his grade, the teacher does not give a grade. Evaluation is important, and a great amount of time will be spent discussing it in the last chapter.

Teacher Evaluation

During your first few years of teaching, you will be evaluated by various members of the staff, since a decision regarding tenure is usually made after three years in a school system. This evaluation should be based in part upon your teaching effectiveness. The person in the school in charge of instruction or supervision will probably be the one who will observe you at various times during the year. This supervisor should be a person who can aid you in becoming a better teacher. His comments should be constructive and help you improve your teaching style.

In various states, you might start teaching without having had student teaching. Student teaching is when the prospective teacher is assigned to a master teacher, in the same specialization, for a number of weeks of "practice teaching." If you enter teaching without student teaching, you might have to enroll at a local college or university for an in-service certification program. Some colleges then provide a teacher educator who will assist you for a period of time in supervised teaching. In any event, such experiences should be helpful to you in your teaching career.

You can attempt a number of lesson or self-evaluation techniques yourself as a way of improving your instructional ability.

1. *Audio tape record* some of your lessons. Place the recorder out-of-sight of the students and audio tape a lesson. Later, after class or in the evening, listen to the tape and do a self-evaluation. You can listen for technical errors or possible voice characteristics of which you were not aware.
2. *Video tape record* some of your lessons. If your school has a video tape recorder (VTR), arrange for one of your lessons to be taped. Later, review the tape and do a self-evaluation. You will find it an interesting experience to see and hear yourself. The new VTR equipment does not need special lighting and can, in most cases, be done right in the shop or laboratory.
3. *Observation* by a fellow teacher can be helpful to the new or inexperienced teacher. You might ask various fellow faculty members to observe and comment on your teaching style. They will probably be

shocked when you ask them to sit in, but the experience can be worthwhile for both of you.

4. Ask your *students* to evaluate or comment on your teaching characteristics. The students are the ones who must listen to you every day, and their suggestions should be given serious consideration. Ask for their comments on some suitable type of questionnaire. Do not ask them to identify themselves on the questionnaire. This technique can and does work if you approach it in the proper manner.

5. Administer a surprise *test* (not for score) immediately after one of your regular lessons. Ask a number of questions directly relating to the lesson content. This will give you a basic idea as to what points of information were retained by the students. Even after what you considered an excellent lesson, the results might be shocking.

School Forms and Paper Work

You will find that classroom teachers have a certain amount of paper work to handle during the normal school year. A school is a large operation and as such, a certain amount of control and organization is necessary to keep things moving along as smoothly as possible. This operation depends upon the cooperation of teachers and students.

It will be to the new teacher's advantage to become acquainted with the various forms that are necessary. It would be best to do this before school begins, rather than after the school year starts.

When the central office puts a due date on a certain form, please try to comply with the request. Your organizational system and personal work schedule will have to be adjusted to keep up with the necessary paper work. Good organization on your part will cut down on the time needed for paper work and other details associated with being a teacher.

Each school system has its own records and school forms. It would be almost impossible to show and list all the forms that a teacher might be requested to use. A few examples of the more common forms will be presented along with a brief description of their use.

The emergency information card (Figure 2–1) is one of the most important records a school is required to have. It is used by school personnel in the event of sickness or accident on the part of the student. It indicates a phone number where either parent can be contacted in the event of an emergency. It also indicates the family physician and dentist.

The classroom or homeroom teacher who is responsible for having the students take the cards home for the parents to sign, should impress

Middlesex County Vocational and Technical High Schools

☐ East Brunswick　　☐ New Brunswick　　☐ Perth Amboy　　☐ Woodbridge

EMERGENCY CARD

Name of Student _____ Grade _____
　　　　　　　　　　　　Last　　　　　　　　First

Home Address _____ Phone _____
　　　　　　　　　　Street　　　　　　City

Father's Name_____ Place of Employment_____
　　　　　　　　　　　　　　　　　　　　　　　　Phone _____

Mother's Name_____ Place of Employment_____
　　　　　　　　　　　　　　　　　　　　　　　　Phone_____

Physician's Name_____ Address_____

　　　　　　　　　　　　　　　　　　　　Phone_____

Dentist's Name_____ Address_____

　　　　　　　　　　　　　　　　　　　　Phone_____

Responsible adult who will care for child if parent or guardian cannot be contacted

Name_____ Address_____ Phone_____

Name_____ Address_____ Phone_____

see reverse side

Does student have any allergies?_____
　　　　　　　　　　　　　　　　explain

Date of last tetanus_____

We urge you to avail yourself of the protection afforded your son-daughter
through school accident insurance.

In the event of extreme emergency, permission is hereby granted to transport
my child to the nearest hospital. I will assume responsibility for payment of emergency care.
Permission is hereby granted to call family physician.

_____　　Signature _____
　　　　Date　　　　　　　　　　　　　Parent or Guardian

FIGURE 2–1

Emergency Card

the importance of this card on the students. The teacher should check the cards as they are returned for accuracy and completeness.

The pupil's daily schedule is recorded on the Pupil's Daily Program card (Figure 2–2), and it has two main purposes. First, in the event a student has to be contacted by someone on the school staff, the program card can be used to determine where a student should be at any given time. Secondly, in the event of some emergency or problem at home, a parent might request an early release for the student. The office staff can check the program and locate the student in the best and quickest manner. Teachers and students must be aware of the importance of this card. The student should take care in filling out the program, and the teacher should check for completeness.

Time	Pe-riod	MONDAY		TUESDAY		WEDNESDAY		THURSDAY		FRIDAY	
		Class	Rm.	Class	Rm.	Class	Rm.	Class	Rm.	Class	Rm.
	1										
	2										
	3										
	4										
	5										
	6										
	7										
	8										
Home Study											

PUPIL'S DAILY PROGRAM

Name_____ Class or Grade_____

Locker No._____ Home Room_____

FIGURE 2–2

Pupil's Daily Program

Attendance laws and regulations vary state to state. The attendance card shown in Figure 2–3 is but one type used in one school district. School attendance is usually taken during an administrative period known in most schools as homeroom period.

The teachers assigned as homeroom teachers are responsible for keeping and recording an accurate listing of the students' attendance. Some states require a state attendance register to be maintained. It is a very important document since state aid in terms of dollars usually depends on student attendance at school.

The attendance card (Figure 2–3) has spaces for daily attendance and monthly totals at the end of each month. The information from this card would then be placed on the official district attendance record.

You will have to consult your school's *Teacher's Manual* to see how it handles attendance procedures. Use care and be accurate in taking attendance if you are assigned as a homeroom teacher.

Register No._____																																Birth Date_____		
Name															District																	**Class**		
	1	2	3	4	5	6	7	8	9	10	11	12	13	14	15	16	17	18	19	20	21	22	23	24	25	26	27	28	29	30	31	Pres.	Abs.	Tardy
Sept.																																		
Oct.																																		
Nov.																																		
Dec.																																		
Jan.																																		
Feb.																																		
Mar.																																		
Apr.																																		
May																																		
June																																		

FIGURE 2–3

Attendance Card

School policies vary a great deal concerning the payment of student fees and requiring students to pay for materials and supplies. If schools require teachers to handle student fees and money in general, then receipts should be used. In some cases, as seen in Figure 2–4, the money is paid directly to the main office. If you need to handle student fees, use care and the necessary receipt forms.

Student control is very essential and necessary to the operation of a school. It requires the cooperation of both students and faculty. If a teacher is careless about student control, students will catch on and usually make the situation a bad one.

The tardy admission slip (Figure 2–5) is usually issued by a person in the office to students who come to school late. The student takes the form and goes to his scheduled period. He presents the slip to the shop

Date _____

Received from_____

_____ $ ___

for_____

Middlesex County
Vocational and Technical High School
Date_____

Received from _____

_____ $ ___

for _____

_____
Principal

FIGURE 2–4

Student Receipt

Middlesex County Vocational and Technical High School

Tardy Admission Slip

Date_____

Please Admit_____

to _____

_____ Time_____

Note Due:

FIGURE 2–5

Tardy Admission Slip

or classroom teacher and should be admitted to class. The teacher should indicate in his class book how late the student entered the classroom. Students who attempt to enter late and do not have a slip should be told to report to the office for one. It informs the school attendance officer that the student has arrived at school.

Class _____   Date _____

The following pupils were absent this
☐ A. M.   ☐ P. M.

_____ | _____

_____ | _____

_____ | _____

_____ | _____

_____ | _____

_____ | _____

Tardy

_____

_____

_____

Instructor_____

FIGURE 2–6

Shop Attendance Report

The attendance card in Figure 2–3 was for use by the homeroom teacher. The shop attendance report (Figure 2–6) is used by the shop or laboratory teacher to report absent students and tardy students to the office. It is used as a control device. For example, if a student reports to homeroom but skips his morning shop period, his absence would be reported by the shop teacher. The report is usually sent to the office at the end of the normal school day. Whoever handles cases of this type

Time Lost Sheet

Class................. Date:....................

NAME	TIME OUT	TIME IN	TOTAL MINUTES
Sign legibly	Time limit three *(3)* minutes		

FIGURE 2–7

Time Lost Sheet

would notice the fact that the student was in homeroom but skipped his morning shop. The student should be called to the office and asked to explain where he was during the morning. This is a student control device and requires the support of all faculty members to make the system work.

The time lost sheet (Figure 2–7) is another student control device. If a student, during the course of the shop period, has to leave the shop, he is required to sign out on the time lost sheet. Likewise, when he returns, he should sign back in. It must be pointed out that the student requests permission of the instructor before signing himself out. The instructor should know where every student is at all times. In the event a student was needed in an emergency, a teacher could be in an embarrassing situation if he did not know where one of his students was at that moment.

```
PERMISSION TO VISIT THE GUIDANCE COUNSELOR



STUDENT'S NAME_____ CLASS _____

DATE_____ TIME_____

INSTRUCTOR_____
```

FIGURE 2–8

Permission to Visit the Guidance Counselor

Some schools require a special type of form for students who desire to see their guidance counselor. Figure 2–8 is a form which can be made out by the instructor giving the student permission to see his counselor. Since many counselors work on a schedule basis in seeing students, it is possible the student will return to the shop and be instructed to report back to the counselor at another time.

A counselor who wants to see a student would make out the permission slip and have it given to the student during homeroom period. At the correct time, the student would show the slip to his classroom teacher and be excused from class. When the student leaves the counselor, the time should be indicated on the slip which is returned to the classroom teacher.

The exact procedure used in your school may vary somewhat from that indicated above. The important thing to remember is that this is another control device to insure the smooth operation of the school.

VISITOR'S PASS

This Pass will admit the bearer

_____

TO _____ *Dept.*

GOOD ON THIS DATE ONLY

Date _____

_____

Principal

To be taken up by instructor and returned to office.

FIGURE 2–9

Visitor's Pass

State laws vary concerning the control of visitors in schools. Most schools have a sign on the door or wall instructing all visitors to report to the office. In some states, failure to do so is a legal violation, and the person is subject to fine.

After reporting to the office, and if need be, the person is issued a visitor's pass (Figure 2–9) and allowed to carry on his business. Upon completion of the visit, the pass is returned to the office.

This is a control device to keep undesirable people out of the school setting. A teacher, upon seeing a youngster of school age he does not recognize, should check into the situation. Likewise, adults not associated with the school should have a visitor's pass with them while in the school building.

Vocational educators have long recognized the value of industrial visits commonly called field trips. Students are taken by bus from the school to the plant or location at which the visit is to be made. The purpose is to acquaint the students with the actual industry being studied in the school shop.

Most schools use some type of permission slip which must be signed by a parent before the student is allowed to go on the field trip. The

---

FIELD TRIP PERMIT

Date_____19____

Name _____

has my permission to go with the_____grade

pupils of the_____

school·on a field trip to_____

_____

on_____19____
       Date

_____
                      Parent's Signature

Approximate time of return will be_____

FIGURE 2–10

Field Trip Permit

basic purpose is to inform the parents that the student will be out of the
school building on a field trip. The school, of course, is still responsible
for the safety and well being of the student while he is on the trip.

The shop teacher making plans for the trip should make sure the necessary forms are completed by the students. A typical example of a form used is shown in Figure 2–10. The teacher should collect the forms and make sure he has one for each student going on the field trip.

REPORT OF MISCONDUCT

Name........................Room............Date........ .....

Nature of Offense............... ....

....

. ...

Disposition of Case........ ....

....

....
Teacher's Signature

FIGURE 2–11

Report of Misconduct

Student control and proper behavior is the concern of every administrator and teacher in any school. Shop teachers, just as any teacher, should try to handle behavior problems by himself and not refer every problem case to the office. However, most teachers will have a problem sometime which has to be referred to the administrator in charge of discipline cases. Some form of office referral or report of misconduct (Figure 2–11) is usually used in most school systems. The teacher writes out the report and sends it with the student to the office. It is a good idea for the teacher to go to the office as soon as possible to check on the outcome. However, never leave your shop or laboratory class unsupervised for even a minute to take a student to the office.

Whenever you use an office referral, make sure you follow-up on the outcome of the case. Use office referrals only as a last resort. Handle as many problems as possible yourself. But remember to always be firm, fair, and consistent when dealing with your students.

Close contact between the school and home is essential to insure the best educational system possible. At times, it may be necessary for the teacher to request a conference with the parents of certain students. The

INTERVIEW REQUEST

Date_____ 19____

To the Parent or Guardian of:

_____ Room_____

Name of Pupil

_____

Address of Pupil

For the best interests of your son-daughter we ask that you call at the school personally, as soon as possible, to confer with the undersigned.

It is our aim to stimulate and direct the growth of each pupil physically, mentally, and socially; and to help the home in building and securing desirable character habits of study and attitudes in the pupil. Only by working together can we secure the right conditions essential to proper growth and development of your son or daughter.

If a pupil's progress is below the desired standard, a conference is requested. The most convenient time for such a conference is

_____

Kindly bring this slip with you

Yours respectfully,

_____ School

_____ Principal
Teacher

_____

Date of interview_____ 19____

With whom_____

Remarks _____

_____

_____

FIGURE 2–12

Interview Request

Middlesex County Vocational and Technical High Schools

PRODUCTION WORK

New Brunswick____   Woodbridge____   Perth Amboy____

Month_____19____   Department_____

SHOP ORDER NO.	QUANTITY	DESCRIPTION	ACTUAL CHARGE	APPROXIMATE VALUE

MR-8

FIGURE 2–13

Production Work

interview request form shown in Figure 2–12 is one technique to inform the parents of the need for such a conference. Such a form may be signed by the teacher or principal, depending upon the nature of the conference.

If the shop teacher desires such a conference, it would be wise to make a carbon copy of the request and leave it with the student's guidance counselor. This way, if the parent fails to come in or call, the carbon copy can remain in the student's folder as an indication that the request was made.

School policy varies concerning production work in the shops. Many shop teachers are glad to take on production work if it is applicable to the types of learning experiences taking place at that time. However it is hard to justify work which does not fit into your teaching schedule, so do not be afraid to say "No" to such requests.

One type of production work form is shown in Figure 2–13. Most forms require the approval of the principal or department chairman. Check your local school policy and procedure before undertaking any production work.

There are many other types of forms which will be used in your school. Those discussed in this chapter are some of the most typical and were presented only as examples. You should become acquainted with those used in your school.

DISCUSSION QUESTIONS

1. As a class project attempt to develop a statement of philosophy for a vocational-technical high school which would be acceptable to all the members of the class.

2. As a class, divide into three or four small groups. Discuss the advantages and disadvantages of the various grading methods suggested in this chapter. Make two lists, one stating advantages and the other stating disadvantages of the three methods. What method of evaluation would your group suggest as the most suitable one for vocational-technical education?

3. Discuss the professional staff guidelines of a local vocational-technical high school. List both the strong features and weak features of the guidelines that are under discussion.

ASSIGNMENTS

1. Obtain a copy of the grading method instructions used in a local school. *As a parent*, discuss the relative strengths and weaknesses of the system. Now, consider yourself *a student*, and repeat the procedure.

2. One of the suggested assignments in the first chapter involved a statement of the objectives of a local vocational school. With these as a start and with the material already discussed, write a series of objectives as you see them, for a vocational school.

3. What forms and records will you, as a shop teacher, be required to keep? What other forms and records, although not required, would be helpful to a new teacher?

ADDITIONAL REFERENCES

American Vocational Association, *Definition of Terms in Vocational, Technical and Practical Arts Education.* Washington, D.C.: American Vocational Association, 1964.

American Vocational Association, *New Designs in Vocational, Technical and Practical Arts Education in the Public Schools.* Washington, D.C.: American Vocational Association, 1968.

Association for Supervision and Curriculum Development, *Educating the Children of the Poor.* Washington, D.C.: Association for Supervision and Curriculum Development, 1968.

Association for Supervision and Curriculum Development, *Theories of Instruction.* Washington, D.C.: Association for Supervision and Curriculum Development, 1968.

Draper, Dale C., *Educating for Work.* Washington, D.C.: National Association of Secondary School Principals, 1967.

Kidd, Donald M. and Gerald B. Leighbody, *Methods of Teaching Shop and Related Subjects.* Albany, New York: Delmar Publishers, Inc., 1966.

Mager, Robert F., *Preparing Instructional Objectives.* Palo Alto, California: Fearon Publishers Inc., 1962.

Mager, Robert F. and Kenneth M. Beach, *Developing Vocational Instruction.* Palo Alto, California: Fearon Publishers Inc., 1967.

Rose, Homer, *The Instructor and His Job.* Chicago: American Technical Society, 1966.

Silvius, G. H. and E. H. Curry, *Teaching Successfully in Industrial Education.* Bloomington, Illinois: McKnight & McKnight Pub. Co., 1967.

Trump, J. Lloyd and Dorsey Baynham, *Guide to Better Schools.* Chicago: Rand McNally & Co., 1961.

Chapter 3 SHOP ORGANIZATION AND MANAGEMENT

The shop or laboratory teacher, by the nature of his assignment, will spend the major part of the teaching day in a shop or laboratory. Shop teachers need more organizational and management skills than English, mathematics, and social studies teachers do. This does not mean in subject matter, but rather in facility management and organization. There is a great deal more involved in a shop situation than in an academic classroom. Therefore, the new shop teacher will want to spend some time in his shop before the first day of school.

It would be nice if school districts would *require* and *pay* shop teachers, especially new ones, to come in a week or two before school starts to organize the shop. This, unfortunately, will probably not be the case. However, the new teacher might make such a suggestion upon being employed. Even if the answer is "No" you might still consider spending a week organizing the shop to suit your needs. Being well organized the first day of school will make you feel comfortable and certainly better prepared to meet your students.

Many books have been written about shop organization and management and much has been written about designing and planning new vocational-technical facilities. Chances are that you, as a new teacher, will not be asked to plan a new facility during your first year of teaching. If you are, consult the references listed at the end of this chapter.

This chapter is written mainly as a guide to the new teacher who will be teaching in a shop someone else designed and organized for teaching.

The Physical Facility

One of the most important features of your teaching will be the shop or laboratory. The physical plant, as it is sometimes called, is part of the learning environment, and you should do as much as possible to make it attractive to the students. Ask yourself the question, "Will the students want to work and learn in the shop atmosphere?" The impression left with the student when he enters the shop for the first time is important. This does not imply a home-like atmosphere of comfort, but rather an industrial atmosphere designed for work, as attractive as can be for the particular specialization. You should try to achieve a physical plant that causes students to say, "Let's go to work."

Your primary concern should be the safety of the students in your shop. It is your responsibility as the teacher to be concerned with the physical well-being and safety of the students in your class. The physical layout of the shop should be such as to provide safe work areas, walk zones, and independent study areas. Any experience from industry should be helpful in this area.

The placement of equipment and machines should be such as to promote safe walk areas in the shop and a work area around each piece of equipment. Be concerned with the traffic areas of the shop. Is there sufficient walk space to the tool panel and the storage areas in the shop? Does student movement in the shop cause unsafe working conditions for some of the work stations? Is there sufficient work space for each student and for every work station?

Another important physical facility is the instructional area or center. The total shop facility, of course, is used for instructional purposes, but is there an area which can be used for formal lesson presentations? One of the most suitable instructional areas would be a small classroom adjoining the shop with glass separating the two. The glass wall between makes it possible for students to be at work in the shop while others are engaged in independent study or research in the instructional classroom. The teacher, while in the shop, is able to see what is going on in the instructional classroom. This is perhaps the ideal situation, but you might not be in such a situation. In that case, attempt to develop a lecture area within the shop. You would need proper seating facilities, a chalkboard, and a movie screen and shades to darken the area for slides and movies that might be shown to the students. Make the instructional areas as comfortable as possible both for the students and for yourself.

Color can add to the appearance of your shop. It can also be used to outline safety zones, work areas, and walk zones by means of lines painted on the floor. Color coding of tools and safety devices on machines and equipment can be a useful control device as well as a safety feature in your shop. If you find yourself in an old shop, the addition of some paint may help to improve its general appearance.

A daily concern of every teacher should be heating, lighting, and ventilation. You should make every effort possible to assure the comfort of your students. Good lighting is necessary both for the safety and accuracy of the work the students are engaged in. A certain amount of fresh air is needed even on the coldest day. Your attention to these small details will help to develop a proper facility for the teaching-learning situation.

If you are involved in planning a new shop facility, seek expert advice from someone engaged in shop planning activities. New facilities should be designed which are flexible to the changing needs of a technological society. The most up-to-date shop of today may be outdated in five or ten years if flexibility of design is not considered during the planning stages. Wide open spaces with movable or flexible walls seem appropriate for modern shops. Electrical grids in the floor assure the portability of equipment and machines. A concern with the emerging occupations of tomorrow should be our concern in planning the shops for today's schools.

Equipment

Of main concern to the teacher will be the adequacy and safety features of the shop equipment. Make sure you check out each piece of equipment for proper operation as well as safety features before allowing students to operate it. It is your responsibility to maintain the equipment and insure that the proper safety guards or features are operational. Students, likewise, should be instructed to report any damaged equipment immediately to the instructor.

It is the teacher's responsibility to make sure the necessary preventive maintenance is performed on the equipment as stated in the instruction booklet. It is wise to keep a maintenance log book for each piece of equipment. Students can and should be assigned to do the maintenance after having received proper instruction, but it is the instructor's responsibility to make sure it is properly done.

The teacher is also responsible for equipment repair. If the repairs qualify as a learning experience for the students, then they can be done during class time. If not, then the instructor can do the repairs after class, or request an outside source to do them. Always remember your major function is that of an instructor and not a repairman.

You may want to consider color coding of the equipment. This might be as simple as red paint on the safety guards and green paint on the control functions. Markings on the floor may be used to indicate the work zone of the machine operator. No one but the operator would be allowed in the work zone at any one time. This tends to keep two students away from any piece of equipment at the same time and is a safety feature.

How the equipment is placed in the shop is important. As a new teacher in an old shop, you might not have much control over equipment location. At least give the lay-out a fair trial before requesting any major movement of wiring and equipment.

Establish a priority listing of new equipment or replacement needed to keep your shop up-to-date with modern industry. Do not be afraid to ask for new equipment, but be able to justify the need for new or replacement equipment.

Hand Tools

Students should be instructed to report any unsafe or damaged hand tools to the instructor, but it is the instructor's final responsibility to make sure that the tools are in safe operating condition. It is a good idea to have some system of marking or color coding tools so as to identify in what shop they belong. Some tools of a special nature will be found in only one shop, but others may be common to more than one shop. Color coding or marking is a good tool control device and should be helpful to the smooth operation of the shop.

Hand tool storage can be a problem. Many shops still use tool cribs and as a student needs a tool, he checks it out of the tool crib. Other shops may have tool cabinets or storage areas which are available to all students. Some form of daily inventory must be used with either system. Each week, a different student should be assigned to check the tools at the beginning and again at the end of the class period. Any missing or damaged tools should be reported to the instructor.

If an existing tool crib is used for storage, not much can be done about its location. If tool storage cabinets or wall panels are used, some portability may exist. The tool storage area should be easily accessible for everyone in the shop. However student movement in this area should not cause unsafe working conditions.

If a tool crib is in the shop and you decide to have a student sign out tools, make the experience a learning one. Can you justify having a student spend two or three hours per day in the tool crib? If your answer is

"Yes," at least make sure that the tool crib assignment is rotated on a weekly basis.

The instructor is responsible for the repair or replacement of defective hand tools. A tool inventory at the beginning and end of each school year can be helpful. Each year, order tools to replace those lost or damaged during the past school year.

Depending upon the shop you are teaching, students might request to borrow various hand tools for home use. Before loaning tools, it would be wise to check with the principal if any school-wide policy exists dealing with the subject. If you are allowed to loan shop tools on an overnight basis, develop a shop loan slip that the student makes out and signs. It should state what tool he is taking, the date it will be returned, and if damaged or lost that he would replace it.

Supplies

The ordering, storage, and inventory of supplies is another task faced by the shop teacher. Most vocational schools require teachers to submit an annual order for their particular shop. In addition, it is usually possible to submit smaller purchase orders during the normal course of the school year. However, it is usually to the best advantage of all parties if the needs for the total school year can be anticipated in advance and ordered on the annual order.

If you maintain a monthly inventory of supplies, it should be easy for you to anticipate the demand for various items. Your inventory sheet actually becomes a "needs" list and makes the preparation of your annual order a less demanding task.

Maintain the security of all your supplies. It is a good idea to keep them under lock and key when you leave the shop. Your policy concerning student use of supplies should be made very clear to the students early in the school year. Are the students allowed to take supplies directly from the storage area? Are the students supposed to ask the instructor for supplies? Whatever your decision or policy is in regard to supplies, make sure you stay consistent in the enforcement of the policy.

Lecture Area

Many times, lesson presentations in the shop involve a demonstration on a certain machine or special piece of equipment. At other times, lessons and class discussions are carried on in a more formal setting in a lecture area of the shop. It is suggested that you set up a lecture area within the shop, if an attached classroom is not available for your use. The best situation seems to be when a classroom is attached to the shop and divided from it by windows. This allows the teacher to be in the shop but still able to supervise students involved in report writing or research in the classroom.

In the event your lecture area is in the shop, you can still do a number of things to assure it of being a suitable instructional area.

Adequate seating facilities for all students should be provided. Do not require the students to sit on work benches during your lesson and discussion periods. The seating that is provided should be of such a nature that it is movable and has suitable space for writing. Make sure that the seating area is designed so that students will not have to face a window area in the shop. The most favorable would be a seating arrangement in which the window area was to the left or right of the seating area. Adequate chalkboard and bulletin board space should be available in the lecture area.

You will want to use visual aids from time to time during your presentations. These visual aids might include the use of the overhead projector, filmstrip projector, slide projector, and movie projector. If you plan to use visual aids often enough, it is reasonable to request that a permanent screen be provided in the lecture area. In addition, window shades or blinds on the windows are needed to darken the shop.

You will need some type of bench or movable cart to store your lecture materials on during the presentation. This bench or cart should be positioned so that all students have good visibility.

As you start using the lecture area, you, no doubt, will want to make various modifications for improvement. Ask your students for their reactions. Ask them for recommendations that might result in a still better lecture area. After all, you as the instructor see only from one side of the desk, the students observe from the opposite side — the most important side.

Shop Safety

It is essential that you are prepared on the first day of school with a list of safety rules or regulations. Do not allow the students to start any shop work whatsoever until after some basic instruction in safety procedure has been given to them.

The list of rules may be general safety regulations that apply to all shops and laboratories in the school and in addition, specific regulations for your shop or laboratory. It is possible that a set of rules of the general type has been developed and is used by all teachers in the school. It is suggested that you be well informed about your school's procedure concerning shop safety regulations.

No one list of general shop rules will meet the requirements of all schools or all shops. You may want to consider the following rules in developing your own list.

1. Do not run in the shop.
2. Do not throw any object in the shop.
3. Report all accidents, no matter how minor to the instructor immediately.
4. Always wear the proper eye glasses or shields as required by law and your instructor.
5. Never use a machine without the approval of your instructor.
6. Never ask your instructor to operate a piece of equipment on which you have not received instruction.
7. A business-like atmosphere should exist in the shop. Horseplay will not be tolerated.
8. Clean machines after use.
9. Return unused materials to their proper storage areas.
10. Do not make adjustments on machines while they are in operation.
11. Use appropriate safety devices on the machine you are operating.
12. If in doubt about procedure, or the operation of any machine, check with your instructor.

In addition to the general shop rules or regulations, you should develop a more specific set of rules for your specialization. It is impossible to list all the rules concerning safe work practices in the school shop. Your shop, the level of students, and the kind of instructional activities that go on will all determine the kinds of safety regulations required for a safe shop. An electronics shop will have one set of regulations and the cosmetology laboratory, another set.

Before any student is allowed to work in class, you should review the safety regulations with the students and make sure that they understand them and agree to follow them.

It is a good idea to ask each student to sign a copy of the shop rules indicating that they received instruction on the rules and agree to observe them. The following statement could be used.

I, _____, received shop instruction
                        (name)

on _____, and agree to observe the
                        (date)
shop rules for electronics shop.

You would file the statements and use them if necessary in case of violation of shop regulations. The main value of the statement is that you have a written indication that all your students received instruction on the safety regulations.

A week or so after you reviewed the shop safety regulations you might want to give the students a written test on the safety rules. This has two major values. First, it reviews all the safety regulations. Secondly, you file the safety tests in your files as a second indication of instruction dealing with shop safety.

Shop safety is not something you discuss for one day and forget about the rest of the year. Each day you should discuss it in relation to your demonstrations and lessons. Safety is an ongoing subject, and it is your responsibility as a teacher to impress its importance upon the students.

In recent years many states have passed special regulations concerning eye safety protection. Those states that have laws concerning eye safety in schools, specify when eyeglass protection must be worn and also what type of glass and glasses should be provided for the students. Your local administrator should have a copy of the state regulation concerning eyeglass safety in your state. It is to your advantage and the safety of your students to live up to the state law requirements.

Industry is very concerned with the safety of its employees and spends a great amount of money on accident prevention. You should be able to obtain posters and publications dealing with local industrial safety practices to use in your classes. Display industrial posters in suitable areas of your shop to remind students continually of the importance of industrial and shop safety.

Be sure you understand the school procedure to be followed in the event of accident, injury, or sickness. Every school should have some policy or procedure to be followed in the cases indicated. If you are qualified to administer first aid and do so in an emergency, will you be covered and supported by your local administration? Many schools have a nurse on duty, but precious time may be involved before the nurse is able to get to the shop. The victim may require immediate care. Shop teachers should have some basic understanding of first aid and what care or treatment, if any, would be needed. A statement concerning accidents and injuries should be included in your list of shop rules.

Accident report forms should be available in your school. All accidents, no matter how minor or serious, should be reported immediately. The use of an accident report form provides a definite record of the accident and may be useful in the event of liability involvement against the teacher and school. The teacher should keep one copy and send one copy to the office. In the event your school does not have a regular accident report form, it is suggested that you design a form which includes at least the following information.

1. Name of student
2. Date, time, and place of accident
3. Person in charge at time of accident
4. Nature of the injury
5. Cause of the accident
6. How accident could have been avoided
7. Witness to accident

A concern of many shop teachers is liability in the event of legal action against them, by a student or his parents, in the event of an accident. It would be to your advantage to check with your local administrator concerning board of education policy on teacher liability. The important question is "Are you covered as an individual, by a board of education insurance policy, in the event of a legal judgement against you?" If the answer is "No," you might want to consider a personal liability insurance contract designed especially for shop teachers.

The safety of students is a major concern of all teachers and school personnel. It is both a moral and legal responsibility of everyone involved with schools. The teacher must do more than teach safety — he must practice it and see to it that the students do likewise at all times.

Personnel System

Some form of a student organizational system within a shop or laboratory is usually required and essential for good operation. These systems are commonly referred to as student personnel organizations, personnel systems, or clean-up systems. A system of this nature is usually not needed in a normal classroom situation but is essential to the organization and administration of a shop facility.

The personnel system is a system of assigning students on a rotating basis to various shop assignments. These assignments vary from being a shop foreman to being a sweeper. A structure of organization with a chain of command is used to make the system most workable. Five or ten minutes before the end of the shop period, a signal is given that it is time to clean up and ready the shop for the next class. It is at this point that the assigned tasks of the personnel system are performed by the students. The shop foreman is responsible for reporting to the teacher on a daily basis. The teacher, of course, has the final responsibility for the condition of the shop and should make frequent checks on the operation of the personnel system.

The personnel system is of value to the teacher as well as the students. The teacher benefits in that it provides him more time to work with individual students and gives him time to get organized for his next class. The students benefit from being part of an organizational system designed to accomplish a stated purpose. The students should gain some administrative or managerial experience during the period of time they serve as foreman.

The development of a personnel system is a good project and should involve pupil-teacher planning. The most effective system would be one that the students had a part in designing. The teacher would attempt to describe the problem and then ask the students for suggestions.

Various types of systems are designed to administer a personnel system. It is not the intent of this chapter to present a number of systems for your consideration. A review of some recent copies of *School Shop, Industrial Arts and Vocational Education,* and the *Journal of Industrial Arts* should give you some ideas of systems teachers have found workable. The three indicated sources are periodical magazines which are of interest to shop teachers. A well-designed personnel system should have a number of features including the following.

1. A responsibility chain of command
2. A detailed description of each position
3. A rotation technique to assure that each student will have an opportunity to hold all positions during the course of the school year
4. An assignment every week for each student

The success of the personnel system will depend to a large extent on the planning that went into its design. It will also depend on how well the teacher explains the purpose of the system and the cooperation he receives from the students.

Displays

The importance of shop appearance should be evident by this time. Many factors already mentioned contribute to the total appearance of the shop. You will want an attractive bulletin board, showcase, and wall charts since these add to the total environment of the shop.

A suitable bulletin board display is one that is neat in layout and contains materials of interest to the students. Do not fall into the trap that many teachers do and start the school year with a neat bulletin board and end with the same one. Make an honest effort to at least change the bulletin board display monthly or, better yet, every two weeks. The bulletin board is a good place to put industrial items that should be of concern to your students.

If you have a display case in your shop or in the hall, attempt to place items in it of interest to both students and visitors to the school. It is one way of showing others what type of activities and project work are going on in shop. Again, attempt to change the display at least every month.

Many companies supply wall charts on a free basis to schools. It would be worth your time and effort to request safety charts and instructional charts from industries appropriate to your specialization.

Attractive, well-designed bulletin boards and displays require time to design and put up. The effort or lack of effort you exert will be reflected in the type of program with which you end up.

A few more suggestions for the shop teacher are listed below.

1. Have a clean shop.
2. Have a suitable seating area for all the students.
3. Have an attractive bulletin board display.
4. Have everything in proper order.
5. Have all machinery in good working condition.
6. Have all hand tools in proper storage areas and in a ready to use condition.
7. Have a suitable supply of materials available for use.
8. Have all necessary school forms available for your use.
9. Have proper locker space available for your students.
10. Have examples of class projects or experiments available for student inspection.

DISCUSSION QUESTIONS

1. As a class project, develop a list of general safety regulations which would be suitable for any shop or laboratory.

2. Divide the class into small groups by subject matter specialization. Through small group discussions, develop lists of specific safety regulations for the various specializations.

3. Discuss various designs suitable for a shop personnel system.

ASSIGNMENTS

1. What is your board of education's policy regarding teacher liability in the event of a shop accident?

2. What are the regulations in your state and school concerning eye safety?

3. Design a student personnel system for the shop in which you will be teaching.

4. From periodicals copy samples of tool and/or supply arrangements for use in your shop or laboratory.

5. Obtain a copy of your school's inventory form and order form for supplies and equipment.

ADDITIONAL REFERENCES

American Association of School Administrators, *Planning America's School Buildings*. Washington, D.C.: American Association of School Administrators, 1960.

American Vocational Association, *Area Vocational Education Programs*. Washington, D.C.: American Vocational Association, Research and Publications Committee, 1959.

California State Department of Education, *A Guide for Administrators, Instructors, and Students*. Sacramento: California State Department of Education, 1963.

Englehardt, Nicholas L., *et al. School Planning and Building Handbook*. New York: F. W. Dodge Corporation, 1956.

Herrick, John H., *et al. From School Program to School Plant*. New York: Henry Holt and Company, Inc., 1956.

Hoagland, Donald P., "Safety-Practice Form," *School Shop*, (June 1961), 22.

Holt, E. E., *The Student Orientation and Questionnaire Phase of the Vocational Education Community Survey*. Columbus, Ohio: Division of Guidance, Ohio State Department of Education, 1963.

Hughes, Wayne P., "Eye-Protection Legislation," *School Shop*, (February 1966), 27–29.

Indiana State Department of Public Instruction, Division of Vocational Education, *Planning Shops for Industrial Education Programs*. Indianapolis: Indiana State Department of Public Instruction, Division of Vocational Education, 1956.

Mississippi State Department of Education, *School Shops, Layouts, Justifications and Equipment for Trade and Industrial Education Programs*. Jackson: Mississippi State Department of Education, 1956.

National Council of Schoolhouse Construction, *Guide for Planning School Plants*. East Lansing, Michigan: National Council on Schoolhouse Construction, 1964.

Olsen, Fred A., "Student Injuries and Teacher Liability," *School Shop*, (October 1969), 21.

Sumption, M. R. and J. L. Landes, *Planning Functional School Buildings.* New York: Harper & Row, Publishers, 1957.

Taylor, J. L., *School Sites — Selection, Development, and Utilization.* Washington, D.C.: U.S. Department of Health, Education and Welfare, Office of Education. U.S. Government Printing Office, 1958.

Viles, N. E., *Local School Construction Programs.* Washington, D.C.: U.S. Department of Health, Education and Welfare, Office of Education. U.S. Government Printing Office, 1957.

Williams, William A., *et al. Accident Prevention Manual for Shop Teachers.* A Professional Publication of the National Association of Industrial Teacher Educators. Chicago: American Technical Society, 1965.

Part II LESSON PLANNING

Chapter 4 DETERMINING WHAT TO TEACH

Course content may or may not have already been determined in the school in which you will begin your teaching career. In older, well established vocational-technical schools, the new teacher may be handed a course of study for the class or classes he is hired to teach. If you are provided a course of study and expected to follow it for the year, you may want to modify and improve it. In other situations, the new teacher may be expected to develop a course of study. This may very well come as a shock to a new teacher. A *good* course of study cannot be developed in a few days or even in a few weeks and, to be most effective, it should involve joint planning among teachers and the industrial community.

The material in this chapter will point out some of the basics of determining what to teach. More detailed information can be obtained by using the references that are suggested at the end of the chapter.

The traditional vocational curriculum is usually divided into smaller units which are offered on a semester or yearly basis. If a three-year program in plumbing is offered, it will typically be divided into three one-year courses such as Plumbing I, Plumbing II, and Plumbing III. It also could be divided into six smaller units based on a semester basis and divided into six one-semester courses. As stated earlier, this is traditionally how vocational programs and courses have been established and is not intended as an argument for or against the traditional system. Since most courses and programs are structured this way, the established format will be followed.

Program is defined as the pursuit of a certain specialization such as cosmetology, electronics, etc. *Course* is defined as one segment of the total program. A *unit* is still a smaller sub-division of a course.

It is first necessary to consider the product (student) who is about to enter the vocational program. Secondly, it is necessary to establish some level of behavioral performance to be expected of the student upon completion of a program in his chosen specialization. Thirdly, the sequence of development from the input (when the student enters the program) to the output (graduation) must be carefully broken into small segments which might be called units. The product (student) upon completion of the program, should be evaluated in terms of the stated objectives of the program. Likewise, the program should develop from the most simple to the most complex units in order to achieve the level of behavioral performance stated in the objectives of the program.

Objectives of Occupational Education

Chapter one discussed the objectives of education and those especially concerned with occupational education. Now the subject of the program and course objectives must be considered. Course and program objectives conform to the philosophy of the school which has been agreed upon by the administration, staff, students, parents and, of course, the board of education.

Perhaps it would be helpful to read such statements of philosophy by various schools. The schools and locations have not been identified, but the statements themselves were taken from materials published in formal form by the various schools.

1. Vocational Education

The main purpose of vocational education is to prepare qualified individuals for useful employment.

This is interpreted to mean preparation not only in the hand skills necessary to be successful in any given occupation, but also to develop those traits necessary in becoming a satisfied and productive citizen. Therefore, the goal of vocational education is the development of the student socially, academically and civically.

To accomplish this goal, prospective students should have the following interest and abilities.

1. Interest in pursuing education in a trade in terms of pre-employment training.
2. Ability to profit from the instruction.
3. Meet the entrance tests and requirements that indicate ability to profit from the training.

Vocational high school programs usually provide for one half of the time to be spent in the shop and the remainder in related and academic work. Therefore, it is evident that the shop course is the core of the vocational high school program.

The related subjects of mathematics, science and drawing are scheduled in proportion to their use in the trade being studied. All related subjects have a practical relationship to the fundamentals, and therefore, emphasis is placed on applying those principles.

These programs are approved by the State Department of Education and a vocational high school diploma will be granted to all graduates.

2. Institute Purpose and Objectives

The County Technical Institute offers college level technical programs designed to equip graduates for immediate employment in specialized fields. The programs are so arranged that each student acquires some degree of competence in manual skills, plus supporting knowledge in mathematics, science, English and the humanities. Basic supporting courses are presented in sufficient depth to provide insurance against obsolescence in technology. Graduates will be qualified, either immediately or after appropriate work experience, for such positions as are listed under each program description.

3. General Statement of Phliosophy

The Board of Trustees of the _____ has, as its central purpose and objective, the goal of providing high quality education and specialized skill or technical training for the youth of _____ County who aspire, and are qualified by interest and ability, to prepare for a career in a craft or specialized occupation.

We recognize that implementation of this objective involves interrelation of many functioning parts; the staff, the facilities, the student and the curriculum. We, therefore, shall endeavor, in every way possible to develop an effective blend of all aspects and the several functioning parts recognizing that the key to the success of the total program is the instructional staff, and, hence, the individual teacher.

As one reads the three statements, the philosophies and objectives of the various schools become apparent. Program evaluation should be based upon the statements made. The board of education, administrators, and faculty should stand accountable for the various programs which attempt to meet these broad statements.

The local board of education is responsible for the development of the statement of philosophy and the stated objectives of the school. The teacher is responsible for conforming through his course to the central thrust of the school.

Objectives of Your Course

The instructor, in most cases, stands accountable for determining and stating the objectives of a particular course. It is well to accept the advice of the members of an advisory committee in listing the objectives of a particular course.

Remember, a course is but one part or segment of the learning activities making up the program. If a three-year program in electronics is offered, it will probably, mainly by tradition, be broken into three one-year courses or six one-semester courses. A three-year electronics program might be divided into Electronics I, Electronics II, and Electronics III. The relationship among the three must be carefully determined in advance of the curriculum development effort. The student should be able to proceed from the most simple elements of Electronics I to the most complex items in Electronics III. It is therefore essential that the staff member assigned to teach Electronics I be well acquainted and informed of the relationship between Electronics I and II and III. In simple words, it must fit into the total program.

The program objectives would relate closely to the stated objectives of the school. If the main purpose of occupational education is to prepare qualified individuals for useful employment in a certain specialization, then the major program objective would probably be the same. In a practical nursing program, the primary objective would, no doubt, be to prepare qualified individuals for useful employment as practical nurses. And, likewise, this would be the primary objective of all the other specializations offered in the school. The primary objective of a college entrance program is the preparation of individuals for some form of higher education. The practical nursing program would, or should, be evaluated in terms of the number of graduates who enter the field for which they trained. The college entrance program should be evaluated in terms of the number of students who are successfully admitted to colleges.

The classroom teacher will be mainly responsible for determining and stating the objectives of a particular course. His objectives are, or should be, greatly influenced by the objectives of the school and the program his course is a part of. A student completing the stated objectives of the first course should meet the entrance requirement for the second course. Likewise, the student completing the stated objectives of the second course should meet the entrance requirements for the third and last course. Then, the same student completing the stated objectives of the third course should meet the stated program objectives and be prepared for entry level employment in his specialization.

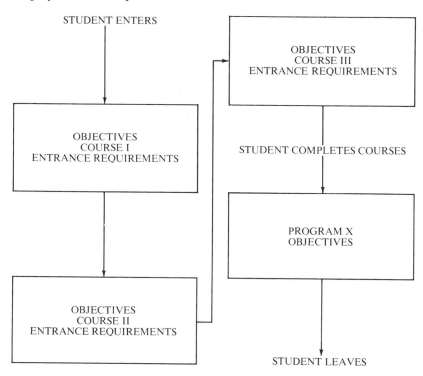

FIGURE 4–1.
Course to Program Relationship

Figure 4–1 shows the traditional sequence of courses used to reach and complete the program objectives. Completing the course objectives of Course II will meet the entrance requirements of Course III. It would be wrong to allow a student to enter Course III without meeting the stated objectives of Course II.

Each course can still be sub-divided into smaller segments called units. The unit method allows the student to move from the most simple to the most complex unit within the individual course. In fact, a total program could be developed on the unit method principle which would eliminate the need for a course structure within the total program. This is somewhat untypical of the traditional approach but still worthy of note and experimentation. The unit approach is simply a means of dividing course content into smaller packages than the traditional semester or year courses. The unit method of course construction will be used in this book, but it will be limited to the course level rather than the program level.

It is suggested that course objectives be stated in behavioral terms in order to let the student and teacher both know when a stated objective has been met. Much has recently been written about behavioral objectives. References are cited at the end of this chapter that will be helpful to the teacher in writing behavioral objectives. A few examples of objectives that require demonstrated behavior on the part of the student follow.

1. *Test* toggle switches, wires, lamps, fuses, tubes, resistors, capacitators, transformers, and potentiometers, and *determine* their serviceability as component parts.
2. *Identify* 75 percent of the time, in a five minute physical inspection, damaged wires, cables, transformers, capacitators, resistors, tubes, and hardware in a typical power supply.
3. Given the audible output from a normal or defective amplifier, the student can *describe* the tonal quality in terms such as normal, A.C. hum, motorboating, etc.
4. Given the audio amplifier, multimeter, and technical manual, the student can *measure* the ripple voltage to within 10 percent of the value and always know when the ripple is excessive.

It takes time to write suitable behavioral objectives, but the effort will be well appreciated in the long run. Final evaluation should be based upon the stated objectives and necessary records maintained, so that both the student and teacher know what progress is being made.

A well written objective should state the *conditions* and the *criteria* level of acceptability. A student should know when he has met the criteria level of acceptability (performance) and then be able to move on to the next objective.

Curriculum Advisory Committee

The shop or laboratory teacher will want to develop a working relationship with the local industrial and trade leaders within his teaching specialization. In addition to the informal relationship that is desirable some formal relationship should exist. A curriculum advisory committee made up of members of the industrial community can provide such a formal relationship.

Some well established vocational schools will have working curriculum advisory committees for each program, and the new teacher will more or less work with the existing group. However, individual committee members usually serve a one or two-year term, and new members are appointed to replace the retiring members. If you start your teaching career in a brand new vocational center, you will probably be involved with the responsibility of selecting the members for an advisory committee.

The principal may have a total program curriculum advisory committee with whom he works. One of the members from each of the specialized subject committees should be represented on the principal's committee. The laboratory or shop teachers would work with a small committee of perhaps six or eight members who have expertise in a certain specialization such as carpentry. If a school is of sufficient size to have more than one laboratory or shop instructor in a certain specialization, then all the teachers in the specialization would work with a common committee. In other words, a curriculum advisory committee should exist for every program that is offered in the school district.

The committee should be more than a paper committee and be made an active, functioning group. They must feel needed as well as important. A curriculum advisory committee should be of real value to the teachers as well as the students. Their main responsibility should be in keeping the various courses and programs up-to-date with modern industrial practices. Their advice should be considered regarding the purchase of new, up-to-date, machinery and equipment.

If you are faced with the task of developing a course of study, try to involve your curriculum advisory committee early in the developmental phase. They should be a valuable sounding board for your ideas and plans.

Scope and Sequence

Scope and sequence refer to the depth and order of subject matter content. In traditional programs, a logical sequence would be: Drafting I, Drafting II, Drafting III, etc. It is feasible that the drafting program could be divided into fifty or more smaller units and placed in a logical sequence. A student might move from unit to unit at his own pace. This is called "self-pacing."

Scope would refer to the depth and variety within the individual unit. The content of the individual unit would be the determining factor influencing the scope of the unit.

Figure 4–1 may be used as a practical example of scope and sequence. The various courses indicated I, II, and III taken in logical order would be the sequence. The content of each course would be the scope and, likewise, the content of all the courses making up the program would form the scope of the total program. Basically then, scope refers to the content of the individual courses and may also refer to the scope of the total program.

Traditional programs have usually been divided into convenient semester or year packages. The semester program is designed for about eighteen weeks, and the year program for about thirty-six weeks. No doubt, the only reason for this was to fit the school calendar. This is a somewhat weak reason, no doubt, and perhaps is due for a change. It seems to make more sense to divide the subject matter into smaller units and base the content as much as possible on behavior-oriented objectives for each unit.

The teacher concerned with individual differences and using individualized instruction could make it possible for students to progress at a self-pacing rate. As a student completed the stated objectives and the evaluation of one unit, he would be allowed to move on to the next unit in the sequence. The successful completion of any unit would be based upon some demonstrated competency on the student's part, such competency based as much as possible on behavioral performance.

An example in the area of electronics seems worthy of mention. A traditional electronics program would have a unit on power supplies. A teacher interested in the unit method and self-pacing technique might divide his unit on power supplies into eight or more parts.

1. Half-wave rectifier
2. Full-wave rectifier
3. Full-wave bridge rectifier
4. Half-wave voltage doubler
5. Full-wave voltage doubler
6. Voltage tripler
7. AC to DC converter
8. Silicon controlled rectifier

Industrial Needs

The curriculum advisory committee, which was discussed earlier, is one of the major methods of keeping the school staff informed about the local industrial needs of the area. This does not imply that the major function of the vocational-technical school is to meet the local industrial needs. A well planned vocational-technical curriculum would prepare students both for entry level employment and higher education, at the technical institute, junior or community college, college or university level. However, this is a local school matter which should be stated in the philosophy and objectives of the school.

Since vocational-technical education is charged with preparing students for entry level employment, the school, its board, and staff must constantly be aware of the industrial needs of the community. The staff should be fully aware of the local industrial scene, and the various teachers fully informed of the industrial needs in their specialization. Three items seem worthy of note.

1. Seek the *advice* of local industrial and trade organizations. Key personnel should be asked to serve on the various curriculum advisory committees. Curriculum evaluation should be an on-going activity of the various committees.
2. Staff members should be fully informed regarding the industrial *needs* of the community. The needs referred to apply to the number of personnel required and the preparation needed for entry level employment.
3. Discover what *skills* are needed by the students seeking employment in the local industries. This information regarding skill level should be of the utmost concern to the shop and laboratory teachers. If possible, encourage the local industrial leaders to state the skills in terms of performance objectives required for employment.

Cooperation between the school and industry is essential if a meaningful program is to exist. School personnel should take the initiative in establishing such a relationship and continue to make it an active involvement and not just another paper committee.

Pressures of Society

The influence of the good life and pressures from society are on all of us. Public schools and their staffs are constantly in the public eye and under the pressure of a modern day society. It is essential that students be prepared to meet the three basic needs of food, clothing, and shelter. Surely then, one of the most basic pressures on the school would be to prepare students for a productive form of employment in the modern world. Employers are mainly concerned with what one can do and the individual's basic skills.

Higher education has been and, no doubt, will continue to be the goal of many people. As long as this is the case, it would seem reasonable to attempt to prepare students for gainful employment as well as not closing the door for higher education. Our programs should be student centered and as much custom-tailored to meet the needs of students as is possible.

Occupational program planners must give considerable attention to the present and future trends in society. National, as well as local, consideration must be regarded in program planning. Some of the major items worthy of consideration follow.

Urbanization
Mobility of the population
Racial integration
Automation
Rapid change
Specialization
Mechanization

The items listed should be noted and investigated in detail to determine the application at the local planning level.

The Student

As you begin your teaching career, remember you are employed to serve the students. Each and every student is an individual and should be treated with the utmost respect and dignity. Many of us refer to the graduate as the product, and truly that is so after graduation. However, before graduation or completion the student should be viewed as the consumer of our services. Just as any service orientated undertaking, those of us in education should attempt to make our services the best and most valuable to our consumers, the students.

Occupational Analysis

A number of different words are used in writing about occupational analysis techniques. Some might say job analysis, others task analysis, and still others, structural analysis. But basically, an analysis technique is concerned with the activities in which an individual in a particular occupation is engaged.

If you are not fully acquainted with a trade or occupation, the best way to make an analysis would be to observe someone actively engaged in that trade or occupation and make note of all activities over a period of time. An observation of this nature would reveal the skills and knowledge necessary to become a successful practitioner.

Many industries spell out the requirements for positions within the organizations in behavioral terms, and naturally they require individuals to have certain skills to hold various level positions.

Basically then, the concern of the shop or laboratory teacher should be to prepare the student with the necessary skills and related technical knowledge necessary for entry level employment in a trade and industry. Therefore, one basic technique of determining what to teach is an analysis of the trade or occupation that you are teaching. You will note a number of references at the end of this chapter which would be of value to you in doing such an analysis.

You should analyze occupations in behavioral terms and then gear your course of study, lesson plans, and daily procedures to the listed behaviors. A possible procedure might include the following.

1. Philosophy and objectives of the school
2. Occupational analysis
3. Active assistance from the advisory committee
4. Develop the course of study based on items 1, 2, and 3
5. Develop daily lesson plans based on the course of study
6. Continual evaluation of the course

The six statements list the basic procedures from the analysis technique to continual course evaluation. It is suggested that the occupational analysis be conducted in such a way as to start with the most simple activity and proceed to the most complex. This will give a much more systematic approach to the procedure and make for less work in constructing the course of study. For example, in preparing to solo (fly alone) an aircraft for the first time, one must first acquire some basic skills. It would be foolish to practice landings if you had not learned and mastered the proper take-off procedures. One should first learn to take-off, fly level, and then master the landing procedure. Proceed from the most simple to the most complex. You would state the tasks to be mastered in behavioral terms.

1. The student pilot will be able to demonstrate the proper take-off procedure.
2. The student pilot will be able to demonstrate the basic turns and level flight required in the landing pattern.
3. The student pilot will be able to demonstrate the proper landing procedure.

The previous example was given for a very special reason. When the flight instructor signs off a student for his first flight, the student is on his own. After the student's first take-off, he is on his own for the rest of the flight which must end in a safe landing, a faulty landing, or a crash.

Although most of us are not flight instructors, the future of many student rests in our control. Occupational analysis is one technique which, when properly used, will help us provide the best form of occupational programs possible.

DISCUSSION QUESTIONS

1. Divide the class into groups of about five students per group. Ask each group to write a statement of philosophy suitable for a secondary level vocational-technical education program.

2. Divide the class into a number of small groups. Ask each group to write a list of suggestions for selecting the members of a curriculum advisory committee for an automotive mechanics program.

ASSIGNMENTS

1. List the objectives, in behavioral terms, for the specialization you are prepared to teach. These objectives may be for the total program or for just the course you teach.

2. Indicate by title the types of people whom you would ask to serve on your curriculum advisory committee. These individuals should relate to the field in which you will be teaching.

3. Review your present course of study. List its strong points and weak points. Can your present course of study be improved?

ADDITIONAL REFERENCES

Fryklund, Verne C., *Analysis Technique for Instructors*. Milwaukee: The Bruce Publishing Co., 1965.

Gagné, Robert M., *The Conditions of Learning*. New York: Holt, Rinehart & Winston, Inc., 1965.

Leighbody, Gerald B. and Donald M. Kidd, *Methods of Teaching Shop and Technical Subjects*. Albany, New York: Delmar Publishers Inc., 1966.

Mager, Robert F., *Preparing Instructional Objectives.* Palo Alto, California: Fearon Publishers, Inc., 1962.

Mager, Robert F. and Kenneth M. Beach, *Developing Vocational Instruction.* Palo Alto, California: Fearon Publishers, Inc., 1967.

McGehee, W. and P. W. Thayer, *Training in Business and Industry.* New York: John Wiley & Sons, Inc., 1964.

McKeachie, W. J. and S. Kimble, *Teaching Tips.* Ann Arbor, Michigan: The George Wahr Publishing Company, 1965.

Chapter 5 THE COURSE OF STUDY

In planning a cross country flight, the pilot will make use of a number of aids in arriving at his final flight plan. The driver planning a long automobile trip on strange roads should review the road map and plan his route. The teacher who cares will also plan well in advance and follow some form of instructional outline in his day-to-day preparation. The teacher's road map should be a well planned and up-to-date instructional outline called a course of study.

It is true that many teachers have courses of study, but some seldom use them in planning their instructional strategy. Many are dust covered and out-of-date with modern technology. Some teachers will not update their courses of study until administrative pressure is placed on them to do so.

The professional teacher will always attempt to keep his course of study up-to-date with modern industry and look for means to improve it. Up-dating of course content should be a continual process and not something that happens every five or ten years. The well constructed course of study should be close at hand and used in weekly planning and lesson plan construction.

The unit method of course construction will be discussed in this chapter. The course of study should be divided into small instructional segments called units. It is suggested that the units be placed in a loose-leaf notebook or binder so that units may be added or deleted as needed. You might want to consider making the individual units available to your students as they progress from one instructional unit to the next. This informs the student about the instructional content of each unit and the method of evaluation that will be used to evaluate his performance. If you attempt to construct your units using behavioral objectives and levels of acceptable performance, the students should receive copies of the various instructional units. The course of study can be as valuable to the student as it is to the teacher.

Definition

A course of study is a comprehensive guideline which, when properly constructed and followed, will aid the teacher and the students in meeting the specific objectives of the course.

It may be constructed for a one-day, one-week, one-month, one-semester, one-year, two-year or longer courses. It is a planning strategy which, when properly used, should result in improved instruction.

It is best to construct a course of study starting with the most simple and progressing to the most complex material or performance expected. In other words, why fragment a three-year program of electronics into three neat packages, each designed for one year? Would it not be best to construct one course of study divided into many smaller units? This would permit the advanced student to progress at a faster pace and perhaps master the equivalent of a year and one-half in one year. A much closer relationship would or should exist among the teachers who instruct the various courses. The student would be aware of the short range and long range objectives of the program that he is in.

Purpose

The course of study is like a road map for the instructor's use in preparing lesson content for his class. The teacher would check the course of study in making his weekly plans and his daily lesson plans.

The course of study along with daily lesson plans is the ultimate. Usually, the course of study is school approved and adopted whereas lesson plans are the teacher's individual property. The new teacher's main problem is to plan what to teach using a course of study and adding lesson plans as the school year progresses.

The course of study is useful in the event of illness to the teacher in that the substitute teacher would have an outline to follow in continuing the instructional process. If a teacher decides to leave his position during the school year, the replacement teacher could carry on along the specified structure contained in the course of study.

It is suggested that the course of study be placed in a loose-leaf binder and kept on the teacher's desk. Students should have a copy made available to them and be encouraged to use it as needed.

Reasons for Using a Course of Study

If the shop and laboratory teachers are not convinced of the value of a well planned course of study, little would be achieved in forcing them to construct one. Teachers must be convinced of the value of a course of study before they construct one.

A number of items must be considered and undertaken before a course of study is constructed. The philosophy and objectives of the school must be considered since they relate to the philosophy and objectives of the various courses of study. An occupational analysis of the occupation (electrician, practical nurse, etc.) would also have to be undertaken. The advisory committee would have been involved from the planning stage on through to their approval of the completed course of study.

After the course of study is approved by the advisory committee and used as the basis for instruction, its relationship to the weekly plan and daily plan must be considered. The primary reason for a course of study is similar to a blueprint or road map that envisions a finished product or destination that one desires to reach. In occupational education, completion of a particular course should result in a level of demonstrable performance on the part of a student. If a student is graduated from a private barber school and passes the state examination, he would have a certain level of demonstrated ability of barbering. The student who passes the federal aviation flight test for a private pilot's license has a demonstrable level of flight proficiency. This does not necessarily mean he can fly a four-engine commercial aircraft, but rather that he can fly an aircraft as a private pilot. Completion of a vocational education course should indicate a level of proficiency on the part of the student. Perhaps the student should be issued a certificate indicating what skills he has mastered as a result of his school experiences.

A course of study should provide a detailed outline of the instructional processes to be carried on in the learning situation. It is as much a guide to the teacher in planning his instructional strategy as it should be to the student in realizing what objectives must be met to complete the program.

Developing a Course of Study

A systematic procedure should be used in constructing the course of study. The following is a suggested procedure.

1. Consider and review the philosophy and stated objectives of the school. With the assistance of your curriculum advisory committee, write a statement of philosophy and state the course objectives preferably in behavioral terms. Take into consideration the age and grade level of your students and their educational backgrounds and abilities. Also, consider the practical elements of the amount of instructional time that will be available and the equipment and facility in which the instruction will take place.

2. An occupational analysis should be conducted at this point with the assistance of your advisory committee. Since the members of your committee might very well be the future employers of your students, let them take part and help in the occupational analysis. What level of performance and what skills are needed by a student to enter the specialization that you are teaching? This is the basic question, and the instructional content of the course of study should result from the occupational analysis.

3. Keep your advisory committee actively engaged from the very start. Do not do all the work yourself, and then ask them for their approval. Make them feel a part of the total effort. Even after they approve the course of study, keep them involved in continual evaluation and updating of the course. As they will be employing some of your students, they will be in an ideal position to evaluate the finished product — the student.

4. Start to write the course of study based on the previously mentioned three items. The technique suggested in this chapter will make use of the unit method of construction. The detailed procedure for the actual course of study will be discussed in detail later in this chapter.

5. Weekly and daily plans should then be constructed based on the course of study. The course of study is a comprehensive outline and should not be too restrictive on the content of the daily plans. It should be flexible enough so that the teacher has some variation in the actual lesson content.

6. Continual evaluation should be undertaken in terms of the stated objectives of the course of study. This evaluation should be an on-going process and should involve employers, students, and the school staff.

THE UNIT APPROACH

The unit approach to course construction is simply a technique which divides the subject content into a number of instructional units. These units or instructional packages, when assembled from the simple to the most complex, would make up the course content. Successful completion of the objectives of the beginning unit would also meet the entrance conditions of the following unit

The ultimate goal would be to construct a number of instructional units with clearly defined behavioral objectives and the necessary evaluation criteria for each unit. Early in the school year the beginning stu-

INSTRUCTIONAL UNIT I
SUBJECT

INTRODUCTORY STATEMENT
The actual introductory statement that will be used to introduce the new unit to the students.

BEHAVIORAL OBJECTIVES
The desired behavior of the students after the completion of the unit. Demonstrated skills that the students will have at the end of the unit.

INSTRUCTIONAL CONTENT
Outline, in detail, of the instructional content to be included in the unit. It will be from this outline that the teacher will develop his lesson plans.

METHODS OF PRESENTATION
The instructional strategy used to present the material to the students. Individual instruction, large group instruction, small group instruction, lecture, programmed instruction, computer assisted instruction, etc.

INSTRUCTIONAL AIDS
A listing of the instructional aids that should be used. Films, slides, tape, T.V. computer assisted instruction, in-basket training, problems, etc.

REFERENCE MATERIALS
A listing of reference books, articles, charts, resource people that could be used for supportive information.

EVALUATION CRITERIA
How the students will be evaluated on their success or failure to complete the unit. Should be based entirely on the earlier stated behavioral objectives.

FIGURE 5–1:

Example Outline of an Instructional Unit

dents could be given a prerequisites test to determine with what unit they should start. As an example, let us say the automotive mechanics program is divided into fifty instructional units. By means of a prerequisites test, some students might be able to satisfactorily demonstrate their proficiency on a number of the beginning units. Perhaps one student has demonstrated a mastery of the first five units. Are you, as the teacher, still going to require him to re-do the first five units, or will you allow him to start on unit six? The answer should be that the student could start work on unit six. This is self-pacing and would require individualized instruction on your part.

The unit method is best suited to this type of instruction and when combined with behavioral objectives and performance evaluation can be a very rewarding experience for both the teacher and students.

After the occupational analysis is completed, those involved in the construction of the course of study would outline in systematic order the tasks one in that trade must be able to perform. The sequence (order) should be such that one unit forms the foundation for the following unit and so on until the stated objectives of the course have been met. However, the well prepared course of study will have more complex material and instructional content surpassing the stated instructional objectives. The purpose of these added units is to make sure the teacher is prepared for the students who complete the stated objectives of the course before the end of the school term. The alternative would be to allow those advanced students to concentrate their efforts on the other subjects they are taking. Unfortunately, it will probably be a long time before such a secondary program is in existance.

The construction of each unit would be based on a number of subtopics. The basic structure of a unit would be as indicated in Figure 5–1.

The same format used to outline the style of the individual units of the course of study can be used for lesson plans as well, though greater elaboration would be needed under the section labeled "Instructional Content."

OCCUPATIONAL ANALYSIS

As indicated in the previous chapter, a number of different titles are used to refer to occupational analysis. An occupational analysis is a technique used to determine the skills needed by someone to be adequately prepared for a certain type of occupation. The level of skill attainment might vary from entry level employment to more advanced positions within the specialization. Members of your advisory committee should be helpful in determining what skills and experiences are essential for someone interested in employment in the particular specialization.

If you were developing a course of study for a service station attendant program, the best way to determine course content would be to first observe a number of "successful" attendants. This observation period might last from one to many days.

A priority would be assigned to those behaviors which are most often required. One of the most basic procedures for a service station attendant is making change for a customer after a sale is made. It would be difficult to place a graduate in a service station position if he lacked this basic skill. It is not a technical skill associated with automobiles, but rather a basic skill necessary for every sale the man makes. It is, however, the type of skill that might be overlooked by someone constructing a course of study, yet if a service station attendant was observed, it would probably be the most often used skill that would be observed.

The occupational analysis should be completed, reviewed, and approved by your curriculum advisory committee before work is started on the course of study. The course of study will be good or bad depending upon the quality and quantity of your efforts in doing the occupational analysis.

This same technique of observation could be applied to any occupation. This procedure is seldom used, but it is the practical way to determine what is expected of a person in a particular occupation. Of course, some skills that are necessary in a particular occupation are seldom used and would not be noticed unless a great deal of time was spent observing. For this reason, expert advice from those closely associated with the particular specialization is usually of value in an occupational analysis.

THE OUTLINE

To be a really usable item the course of study should be contained in some form of loose-leaf binder, so that units can be modified, deleted, or added to as the necessity for change or modification is realized. Also, as lesson plans are constructed by the teacher during the course of the year they can be added to the proper unit in the course of study. It is generally much easier to up-date and modify a course of study assembled in this manner than it would be to change a bound copy.

The following items should be considered essential to every course of study.

1. Title page
2. Introductory statement
3. Philosophy of the school
4. Objectives of the course-desired outcomes
5. Student requirements-prerequisites
6. Length of the course
7. Relationship of course to all-school program
8. Topical unit outline
9. Instructional units
10. Advisory committee statement

Each item of the outline will now be considered in detail.

Title Page.   The title page should contain the following information: (a) course title (Machine Design, Machine Design I, Plumbing, etc.); (b) duration of the course (one-year course of study, three-year course of study, etc.); (c) name of the school; (d) department, and (e) date.

Introductory Statement.   This should be a basic statement in which is explained the reasons why such a course is to be offered. You might mention the employment demand for students who complete such a program of studies. The statement should be in plain, non-educational terminology so that students, parents, and employers can understand what is being said. Note the assistance rendered by the curriculum advisory committee and indicate that the committee has approved the course of study.

Philosophy of the School.   Obtain the board of education's approved statement of philosophy and include it at this point in the course of study. As you are aware, this statement should have guided the total course of study development to this point. If school-wide objectives have been approved by the board of education, also include them at this time.

Objectives of the Course — Desired Outcomes.   This is perhaps the most important item in the course of study. It is necessary at this point that you list in simple language the stated objectives of the course. It is on the basis of these stated objectives that the total course of study, the program, the student, the board of education, the administrative staff, and the teacher must stand accountable. The only fair evaluation of the program can be made on the basis of the stated objectives.

Therefore you should use care in writing objectives for the course of study. Do not list statements that are either too vague, too specific, or too difficult to achieve in the time available. It would be best to write statements that refer to desired student behaviors at the completion of the course.

In the licensed occupations we have excellent examples. An objective of a cosmetology course might state, "Upon completion of this course of study, the student should be able to pass the state board examination in cosmetology." The cosmetology program may consist of only one or two courses of study, perhaps even more. The objectives of each course of study should be consistent with the program objectives and lead to success on the state board examination in cosmetology.

In non-licensed occupations, much more is involved in writing objectives. It might be best to list the desired behavioral outcomes in detail. These would be statements such as the following.

The student will be able to do a complete engine tune-up in _____ minutes, and do it successfully 75 percent of the time.

The student will be able to troubleshoot a transistor radio in _____ minutes, localize the trouble, and do it successfully 75 percent of the time.

The above two statements are only examples, and the percentages would vary depending upon your own criterion measure of successful performance.

Student Requirements — Prerequisites. You should now list the prerequisites necessary for the course. This is comparable to certain college classes for which certain courses are prerequisites. Rather than list courses, it is possible to require a certain level of reading or mathematical ability based on standardized tests.

You should also list any special physical conditions that are desirable and, likewise physical conditions that would prevent a student from finding employment in the specialization.

For example, students with skin conditions should be advised to seek professional assistance before electing a barbering or cosmetology course. This writer is aware of students who have completed cosmetology courses and were never advised that certain skin conditions could prevent them from obtaining a state board license.

Electronics students should be advised that color blindness is a handicap in the electronics industry. This is due to the fact that many electronic components are color coded for identification purposes.

Levels of previous learning are important, but it is also necessary to investigate and spell out physical conditions that are desirable for the specialization for which you are preparing the course of study.

Length of the Course. Indicate the number of days, weeks, months, or years that are usually necessary to complete the course. If you follow some of the previous recommendations and develop one course of study for the total program, this should be so specified. In other words, if your school has a three-year electronics program and develops one course of study divided into units, you should make it very clear that the course of study is for a three-year period based on three consecutive school years. You might indicate the approximate number of units that would be completed each year.

It is difficult to determine instructional time until you have taught the course a number of times. It is best to be over-prepared rather than under-prepared, so have more material in the course of study than is required to meet the stated objectives of the course.

Relationship of the Course to the All-School Program.   Indicate how the course relates to the total school program. You should tell in what ways the course relates to the total learning experience of the student and how it fits into the total curriculum offerings of the school.

Topical Unit Outline.   This is a topical listing of the various units in the total course of study. It should be listed in sequence from the most simple to the most complex learning activities. The unit topic should be listed as well as the major sub-topics of the unit. A typical unit might appear this way in the topical unit outline.

UNIT V: VACUUM TUBES

1. Schematic symbols
2. Construction
3. Classification
4. Electron emission
5. Types of emission
6. The emitter (cathode materials)
7. Directly and indirectly heated tubes
8. Theory of diode operation
9. Plate (anode materials)
10. Fleming Valve
11. DeForrest Theory
12. Testing vacuum tubes
13. Life testing (aging)

In the example, vacuum tubes is the topic of Unit V. Unit V consists of thirteen sub-topics which when taken one by one would cover the objectives of the vacuum tubes unit. The units preceding and following Unit V might be as follows.

UNIT I: Magnetism
UNIT II: Electron Theory
UNIT III: Direct Current Circuits
UNIT IV: Alternating Current Circuits
UNIT V: Vacuum Tubes
UNIT VI: Solid State Devices

Each unit would be broken down into a number of sub-topics, and these together would make up the topical unit outline.

Instructional Units.   Earlier in this chapter the unit approach method was discussed in detail. The units are the most important elements in the course of study since it is from the unit content that the teacher develops his daily lesson plans.

The unit should not be confused with the daily lesson plan. A number of lesson plans would be necessary to cover the content included in the unit. As lesson plans are developed, they could be placed with the proper unit and then modified as needed for future use.

Figure 5–1 indicated the sub-topics that should be included in an instructional unit as well as a brief statement regarding each topic. Each student should be encouraged or required to develop at least one instructional unit and have it reviewed by the instructor.

Advisory Committee Statement. A brief statement by the members of the curriculum advisory committee should be included. The statement should indicate their assistance and the approval of the course of study as well as notation that evaluation of the course will be a continuous process.

DISCUSSION QUESTIONS

1. Discuss the various advantages of using a well designed and well developed course of study versus "following the textbook."

2. Discuss the advantages and disadvantages of the "unit approach" as a technique in the development of a course of study. What other techniques are used in courses of study?

3. Divide the class into a number of small groups. Give each group an actual course of study. Ask them to review the course of study and outline its strong and weak features.

ASSIGNMENTS

1. Conduct and prepare an occupational analysis for your specialization. (Machine design, printing, automotive body, carpentry, etc.)

2. Prepare *one* example instructional unit in the manner outlined and described in Figure 5–1.

3. Evaluate your existing course of study that you are presently using. If you are a pre-service teacher, obtain a current course of study in your specialization and evaluate it.

ADDITIONAL REFERENCES

Fryklund, Verne C., *Analysis Technique for Instructors*. Milwaukee, Wisconsin: The Bruce Publishing Company, 1965.

Grachino, J. W. and Ralph O. Gallington, *Course Construction in Industrial Arts, Vocational and Technical Education*. Chicago: American Technical Society, 1967.

Mager, Robert F., *Preparing Instructional Objectives*. Palo Alto, California: Fearon Publishers, Inc., 1967.

Mager, Robert F. and Kenneth M. Beach, *Developing Vocational Instruction*. Palo Alto, California: Fearon Publishers, Inc., 1967.

Rose, Homer C., *The Instructor and His Job*. Chicago: American Technical Society, 1966.

Chapter 6   PRE-PLANNING

The assumption will be made at this point that you are operating and following the course of study that you either have constructed yourself or were given by the administration of your school. In any event, you should be following an outline or course of study appropriate to the subject and grade level that you are teaching. With the course of study as your "road map" it is now your responsibility to get on with the planning and then the instructional process. It is for you to decide on the instructional strategy to be used in the classroom. Only you will be able to find out what techniques and methods work best for you in the teaching-learning situation.

The phrase "teaching-learning situation" refers to the shop, laboratory, or classroom atmosphere that sets the stage for teaching on the part of the teacher and learning on the part of the student. The conditions that establish the teaching-learning situation are the responsibility of both the teacher and learner. Both should share in the responsibility for making the situation the best possible in order to provide the most favorable teaching-learning situation. However, the teacher, as a paid professional, must stand accountable to the students in providing them with the best instruction possible.

The Value of Good Pre-Planning

Chances are that the teacher who is hired one day and in the shop teaching the next day will have difficulties in adjustment and student control. In some cases, an experience of this nature can lead to a negative response on the part of the teacher and perhaps, the loss of a good teacher to the profession.

As indicated earlier in this book, it would be best if new teachers in a school system could be employed a month or so in advance of the first day of class. This lead time would make it possible to orient the new faculty member to the school and give him time to prepare his course of study, term plan, and lesson plans. Some schools are doing this, and perhaps more will do it in the future.

Pre-planning is essential for any new teacher and most experienced teachers. It insures maximum usage of instructional time during the teaching-learning situation. The teacher who is ill-prepared is guilty of wasting his own time but, more importantly, the time of his students. One minute of wasted time has to be multiplied by the number of students in the class.

Pre-planning is part of the strategy used by the teacher in providing the conditions necessary for the best teaching-learning situation. It begins the moment one signs a teaching contract and ends the day of retirement.

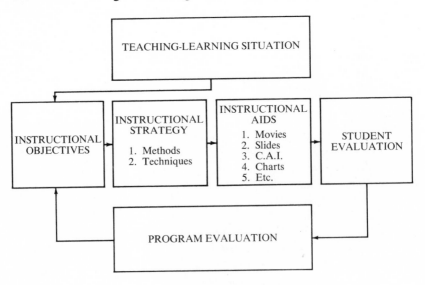

FIGURE 6–1

The Teaching-Learning Situation

It should be an on-going process, and local administrators should provide suitable planning time in the daily schedule of each teacher.

The previous chapter dealing with occupational analysis and the course of study are examples of pre-planning. Now, assuming that a course of study is to be followed, consideration must be given to the plan book, term plan, monthly plan, weekly plan and the daily plan.

Good pre-planning should, and can, prevent embarrassing classroom experiences such as presenting a lesson in ten minutes which you had planned to make in thirty minutes. Pre-planning can avoid your being in the middle of a demonstration and finding that you are missing a tool or instructional device essential to your lesson. Pre-planning can prevent trouble occuring with audiovisual devices that you are using with your lesson. As indicated earlier, it is always better to be over-prepared than to be under-prepared.

The teaching-learning situation is illustrated in Figure 6–1. It really represents what this book is all about. The content of each of the blocks in the diagram will be discussed in detail in this book.

There are five characteristics of good planning:

1. Good planning will be concerned with the abilities, needs, and interests of the students.
2. Good planning will be flexible enough to allow for last minute changes and emergencies.
3. Good planning will be such that a substitute teacher of equal ability could understand and continue using the existing plan.
4. Good planning will outline the instructional strategy (methods and techniques) to be used in the teaching-learning situation.
5. Good planning will constantly show an awareness to the stated objectives of the program and have some method of evaluation built in.

The Plan Book

Most school systems will require faculty members to maintain a plan book of one type or another. A plan book is usually a commercially prepared item which is made available to the teachers. Space is provided in the plan book for the teacher to write out his term plan and weekly plans. The term plan is, as the name implies, the plan for a term (usually twenty weeks). The weekly plan is the plan for one week at a time, and sufficient space is usually provided for a forty-week school year.

The requirements for keeping a plan book vary from school system to school system. One known system requires the plan book to be kept in, or on, the teacher's desk. Plans for at least one week in advance are to be included at any given time. Plan books are to be placed in the teacher's mailboxes on Friday afternoon and kept there until Monday morning.

Any number of reasons can be given for maintaining a plan book. (It results in better teaching, and can be of assistance to a substitute teacher.) But the *teacher* must realize a need in keeping his plan book up-to-date.

Segments are taken from the course of study and included in the plan book. The notation is usually in outline form, but with sufficient references and page numbers to be useful to the teacher or a substitute. The plan book is not to be confused with the daily lesson plan or the course of study. The course of study is the detailed content of the course. The daily lesson plan is the reference source to be followed by the teacher in presenting a lesson. The plan book holds a position between the course of study and the daily lesson plan. In its original condition, it simply has blank spaces for the user to write in his plans, references, and any other notation of value.

In most school systems, the plan books are collected at the end of the school year. They are usually kept on file for a number of years before being destroyed. Plan books may be called in weekly or from time to time by department chairmen or by the administration. Usually the contents are checked for content and pre-planning.

Some plan books also have a section for class attendance and grades. A separate class book for attendance and grades is better than the combined type for two reasons. First, in some schools, plan books are not to be removed from the school. This makes it impossible to take the book home and record grades in it. Second, if plan books are called in, so is the class attendance and grades section of the combination book. Separate books, one for plans and one for attendance and grades, seems to be a flexible arrangement.

The main value of the plan book is to the teacher. Careful planning should make for better teaching and utilization of instructional time. On Monday of each week, review the plans with your students so that they are aware of the week's events. Give them their assignments, if any, on Monday and indicate what day the assignment is due. Remember, the plan book is a tool to help the instructional process, and it will be as helpful as the instructor makes it.

THE TERM PLAN

A section is usually included in plan books designed for writing in the term plan. The necessity for the term plan varies with the course of study. If a well planned, comprehensive course of study is used for the course, an outline type of term plan would be suitable. If the teacher was teaching without a course of study, then a detailed term plan would be essential.

The term plan is a plan for one term of a school year. A term, sometimes referred to as a semester, is usually about eighteen weeks in length.

The term plan, like a course of study, is an example of long-range planning. In a term plan, you should indicate what units will be covered and what level of skill you would expect the students to have mastered at the end of the term.

Assuming that you are using a course of study, the term plan should be no problem. You can simply indicate on a weekly or monthly basis what units from the course of study will be covered in a given period of time. Then, you reference the term plan to your course of study and indicate where the course of study is kept. It is suggested that you keep your course of study on your desk and in plain view of students and visitors. You might want to have a special copy for students and a special copy for visitors.

The teacher operating without a course of study would have to be much more detailed in developing a term plan. But, the term plan could later be used to develop a course of study.

THE MONTHLY PLAN

The monthly plan is simply the plan for one month. It would be considered a long-range plan. The monthly plan would be based on the earlier discussed term plan. The monthly plan can be helpful in allowing the teacher to modify his long-range plans.

THE WEEKLY PLAN

The weekly plan is simply the schedule of the shop activities for a one-week period. It is broken down into five days, and space is provided for the teacher to indicate the shop activities on a daily basis.

The weekly plan is based on the content in the course of study. Individual lesson plans will be prepared by the teacher, based on the weekly plan. For example, if some sort of demonstration lesson is planned for Thursday, the teacher will develop a lesson plan to aid him in presenting the lesson.

Teachers should attempt to make their plans at least one week in advance. In the event of illness, the substitute teacher would have plans for at least one week. Planning much beyond five class sessions is not such a good idea. This is because if the stated material is not covered, a modification in the weekly plan would have to be made, and this would effect the pre-planning.

The weekly plan is short range and is usually presented in the form of an outline of the topics and/or lessons to be covered on a day-by-day basis for a one-week period of time. The instructional strategy (method of presentation) and the types of audiovisual materials to be used should be indicated.

The weekly plan provides for a balance of activities, content, skills, and attitudes in all program areas. It allots time for stressing special interests, allows for unexpected events or developments, and includes working with individuals, groups, and the entire class.

One is not bound inflexibly by exact minutes. One is expected to approximate the time set forth. Include the following in your weekly plans.

> Lesson topics
> Instructional strategy
> Reminders for the week
> Duty assignments
> Audiovisual aids
> Assemblies
> Joint lessons (team teaching, related science, etc.)
> Preparation periods
> Observations (planned visits by your supervisor)

THE DAILY PLAN

The daily plan is the organizational plan of events for one day. It would be based on the normal schedule of activities assigned to a given teacher. It could start with homeroom period and continue through dismissal at the end of the school day. If the school day in the school was based on eight periods, the daily plan would indicate what the teacher was doing each of the periods. The daily plan would be one day of the weekly plan and involves no more planning than that involved in weekly planning.

When the weekly plan is completed, you automatically will have the daily plan for each of the next five school days. The daily plan is in outline form and is not to be confused with the lesson plan. Lesson plans and lesson plan construction will be discussed fully in chapter seven.

Use of the Plan Book

The plan book will be as useful to the teacher as he makes it. It is much like the course of study in that respect. The best course of study is of little value in the back of a file cabinet. Likewise, the teacher who makes satisfactory plans in his plan book but never uses them, will find little value in his pre-planning.

The plan book should be used daily by the teacher and modifications made as required. Students should be informed on Monday as to the plan for the week.

Continual use of the plan book should help guard against repeating the same lesson a number of times or skipping over essential material.

The plans included in the plan book should be based upon the contents of the course of study. Going it alone, without a course of study is not suggested practice but, if it has to be done, it is better to use a plan book and plan as well as is possible, until a course of study is developed.

The plan book is an aid to the teacher in helping plan for the teaching-learning situation. Good pre-planning will usually make the job of teaching an easier one. The teacher who plans from minute to minute and plays it by ear, will usually have a more difficult time than the teacher who believes in and does adequate pre-planning.

Teacher-Teacher Planning

Teacher-teacher planning involves two or more teachers meeting together to plan for the teaching-learning situation. In vocational-technical education such planning should be encouraged between those teachers teaching the same subject. Teacher-teacher planning is also suggested in order to coordinate the instructional program among the shop teachers and the related subjects teachers. The related subjects teachers of mathematics, science, and English should attempt to coordinate their teaching with what is scheduled by the shop instructor.

Joint planning should result in a much more coordinated instructional program, and one that would be of the utmost advantage to the students.

Assignments required of students could be better organized and meet the requirements of two or more teachers. If a research assignment was required by the shop teacher, joint planning might result in the assignment being reviewed by the English instructor for usage, grammar, and style and then passed on to the shop instructor for technical accuracy. The same procedure could be used in mathematics and science courses. Such a program might lend itself to the "team approach" to planning. Teacher-teacher planning makes a lot of sense and should be encouraged by administrators and those teachers who would like to attempt it.

It is essential that teachers have a schedule that would make teacher-teacher planning possible. The administrator who wants to encourage such planning should provide teachers with suitable planning time, office space, and expert advice.

Pupil-Teacher Planning

Pupil-teacher planning provides for, and encourages, student contributions to the development of the instructional process. The teacher and his pupils plan together for topics, units, routines, trips, special events, programs, and projects. Planning can be done between the teacher and the entire class, with small groups or with individual students.

The teacher who has not had experience with pupil-teacher planning should ease into it rather than rush into it blind. Start with small projects involving the students in the planning and then move onto larger projects. Pupil-teacher planning is not something that every teacher can be a part of and want to use.

Planning between the teacher and pupils encourages critical thinking and self-expression. It also encourages the students to be a part of the team in the planning for the teaching-learning situation and thereby, they should feel a closer relationship to the process.

DISCUSSION QUESTIONS

Divide the class into three groups. Assign each of the small groups one of the following discussion questions, and then have a member of each group report back to the class.

1. List and discuss the major advantages of pupil-teacher planning in shop and related subjects.

2. List and discuss the major advantages of teacher-teacher planning in vocational-technical education.

3. List and discuss ways you can involve students in pre-planning activities.

ASSIGNMENTS

1. Develop a weekly plan for the first full week of class, for the subject you are prepared to teach. Follow the format found in one of the commercial type plan books, preferably the type used in the school in which you teach.

2. List the major items of importance to you in pre-planning for teaching your specialization.

3. List the ways you will attempt to involve your students in the planning phases necessary for developing a good teaching-learning situation.

ADDITIONAL REFERENCES

Morse, Arthur D., *Schools of Tomorrow — Today*. Garden City, New York: Doubleday & Company, Inc., 1960.

Rosenberg, Jerry, ed., *New Conceptions of Vocational and Technical Education*. New York: Teachers College Press, 1967.

Skinner, B. F., *The Technology of Teaching*. New York: Appleton-Century-Crofts, 1968.

Tanner, Daniel, *Schools for Youth*. New York: The Macmillan Company, 1965.

Trow, William, *Teacher and Technology: New Designs for Learning*. New York: Appleton-Century-Crofts, 1968.

Chapter 7   THE LESSON PLAN

A lesson plan is an instructional aid for the teacher. The most helpful lesson plans will be those that are prepared by the teacher himself and then put to immediate use in the shop or related classroom situation. Lesson plans prepared by others and then adopted for use will be of limited value to the user. Part of the value of lesson plan construction is the preparation phase of the process. In the preparation phase, the logical sequencing of instructional content should take place, and the instructional aids and media devices selected.

All teachers are able to profit from the use of some form of lesson plan. The most experienced teacher who has taught the same lesson a hundred times only kids himself when he dispenses with using a lesson plan. The first-year teacher presenting a lesson for the first time should have a very elaborate plan to aid him in presenting his lesson. In fact most public speakers and preachers have some form of lesson plan to aid them in logically organizing and presenting their material. A well constructed lesson plan will not save the day for a "poor" teacher, but it can help him. If lesson plans could make anyone a teacher, no doubt, there would be many companies preparing and selling tried and proven lesson plans to the public school systems. There is no substitute for practical ability and know-how on the part of the teacher. The lesson plan is an aid to the teacher and should not be considered a crutch to the poorly prepared teacher.

Policies vary from school to school regarding the preparation of lesson plans. It is possible that you might be employed in a school which requires that daily lesson plans be submitted each day or each week. On the other hand, you might be employed in a school that has no formal policy on lesson plans. Policies mean little, since the important thing is that teachers believe in the lesson plan as an aid to assist them. Forcing teachers to submit lesson plans probably does very little to improve the instructional process, if the various teachers do not believe in the value of lesson plans.

Definition

The teacher should consider lesson plans as management aids in attempting to provide the best teaching-learning situation possible. The plan itself cannot guarantee good instructional presentations, but it should help.

A well prepared lesson plan can also be used as an instruction sheet. Instruction sheets are usually given to the students to assist them in the teaching-learning situation. Lesson plans need not be secret weapons to be used against students, rather they can be used jointly by teacher and student.

Organizational formats of lesson plans vary widely. It is not the style of a lesson plan that is important. What is important is whether the format works in the situation for which it is designed. In most military schools an agreed upon format is established, and all instructors are required to follow the format. There is at least one community college that has an established lesson plan format and requires all evening school instructors to place a copy of their plan in the office each night before their class meets.

The lesson plan format which is suggested in this chapter is one that is compatible to the course of study technique that was outlined in chapter five. It is not a battle to use one style of plan or another. The important thing is to use some form of lesson plan.

An example of the suggested lesson plan format for the Middlesex County Vocational and Technical High Schools is shown in Figure 7–1. The plan format is printed on five by eight inch cards, and the printed cards are available for the teachers to use.

LESSON PLAN
OBJECTIVE INFORMATIONAL

MIDDLESEX COUNTY
VOCATIONAL and TECHNICAL HIGH SCHOOL

LESSON_____ _____CLASSIFICATION_____

OBJECTIVES:

1 _____

2. _____

3. _____

STEP I. PREPARATION

A. Teacher

1. Tools, Supplies, Equipment _____

_____

_____

2. Books, References, Instruction Sheets, Visual Aids_____

_____

_____

B Student

1. Introducing the lesson --- Motivation _____

_____

2. Association or connection with previous lesson_____

_____

_____

STEP II. PRESENTATION Underline methods to be used:

Demonstration, Lecture, Illustration, Discussion, Experimentation

Teaching Points:

1.	6.
2.	7.
3.	8.
4.	9.
5.	10.

STEP III. APPLICATION   Underline methods

Job, Exercise Work, Producation Work, Written Assignment, Oral Quiz, Study Guide

Assignment: _____

_____

_____

_____

STEP IV. TESTING Underline methods

Inspection of Work, Performance Test, Written Questions --- Problems, Oral Questions, List Inspection Points,
Questions, Problems.

_____

_____

_____

_____

FIGURE 7–1

Example Lesson Plan Outline

89

You will find that most lesson plan formats are divided into at least four major areas. These four areas are as follows.

    I.   Preparation phase
   II.   Presentation phase
  III.   Application phase
  IV.   Evaluation phase

A very simple lesson plan format could be established using the four items just listed, and probably prove suitable to most teachers. However, as indicated earlier, this book will attempt to relate the lesson plan construction to the course of study development procedure discussed in chapter five.

The Lesson Plan and Its Relationship to the Course of Study

The course of study represents the total sum of the learning experiences that students will be exposed to within a certain program. Assuming that the course of study was broken down into smaller segments called units, lesson plans would be developed using the outline presented in a unit as a guide to lesson planning.

A unit in a course of study will probably represent an outline of a wide range of instructional content, along with audiovisual aids and various reference sources. The course of study unit would be considered very broad in range as compared to the contents of a lesson plan. The unit structure used in the course of study will determine the number of lesson plans per unit. Also, to a large extent, the ability level of the students will influence the length of any one given lesson. Some units from the course of study might need twenty lesson plans, and others only two. This will depend on how broad an area each of the units attempts to cover. On the other hand, if great depth and planning was involved in the development of the units, the individual units might very well be used as lesson plans. This typically will not be the case and is not advised as a technique.

The lesson plan represents the smallest segment of the material in the course of study. Much greater depth and instructional strategy will be required in the lesson plan as compared to the course of study.

The Lesson Plan and Its Relationship to the Weekly Plan

The weekly plan represents the total plan of activities for the teaching-learning situation for a five-day period. The plan is the schedule of activities under the direction of one teacher. If a teacher instructs two, three-hour classes per day, the weekly plan would be designed for only two classes. This might mean one or two different preparations per day. On the other hand, a related subjects teacher might teach five different groups of students per day and his weekly plan would be designed for five different classes.

One lesson plan might be needed each day for each class for which a teacher is responsible. This might mean two lesson plans for the shop teacher and five lesson plans for the related subjects teacher. Time wise, it is easier to construct two lesson plans than it is five lesson plans. It is probable that some lessons might take longer than the time available, so that one lesson plan might be suitable for two or more days. However, this is a decision that you the teacher will have to make. A lesson plan does not have to be something that is usable for only twenty or thirty minutes of instructional time. It is possible that one lesson might take ten hours to complete. This time would of course, include application of lesson content by the students. As an example, it might take thirty minutes to present a lesson on Ohm's Law, and then one hour to apply the law to various practical problems.

In other words, some weeks you might need five or six lesson plans, and others, not a single one. This depends on your strategy and technique in lesson planning for the teaching-learning situation.

The Lesson Plan and Its Relationship to the Daily Plan

The daily plan is the schedule of activities under the direction of the teacher. The plan indicates the instructional strategy and planning for the day's schedule. The auto mechanics teacher on one day might need two different lesson plans and on another day, none. This all will depend on the type of activities planned for the day. Much of the shop instruction is of an individual nature between the student and instructor, and lesson plans are not generally required in such situations.

Implementing the Lesson Plan

A lesson plan should be of value in a number of ways.

1. Pre-planning for the lesson
2. Logical sequence of presentation

3. As an aid to the actual presentation
4. Information sheet for the students
5. Student evaluation

No doubt, the above list could be expanded to include a few more items. The five stated values of a lesson plan will be more fully elaborated on at this time.

Pre-planning for the lesson.   This will occur if the teacher takes time to prepare a lesson plan. The teacher who walks into the shop or laboratory without a scheduled lesson is apt to be ill-prepared to present a meaningful lesson to the students. Students are able to determine the level of preparation that a teacher puts into pre-planning for a lesson. How many times have you been in a class in which a tool or some item was missing, and the instructor had to stop and search for the missing item? Pre-planning and a good lesson plan can help prevent such embarrassing situations from happening to you.

Logical sequence of presentation.   This does not just happen; it results from thinking out a situation and then putting it into some organizational pattern. In the development of an occupational analysis and then the course of study, a great amount of time is involved in determining the logical sequence of learning experiences. This same systematic reasoning should occur in preparing a lesson plan for your class. If you are attempting to use performance and behavioral objectives in your class, it is essential that all instruction be sequenced from the simple to the complex. This procedure should be followed in the construction of your lesson plans.

As an aid to the actual presentation.   After you go to the effort to prepare a lesson plan, use it during your presentation. It is easy to put it aside and operate without it, but the value of it is lost. This does not imply you read directly from it, rather it implies you follow it much like you follow a road map on a cross country trip. It is an aid, your aid to presenting as good a lesson as possible.

An information sheet for the students.   Some lesson plans will also be usable as information or instruction sheets for the students. Let's say you have prepared a demonstration type lesson plan for hair coloring in a cosmetology class. Why not use it as a handout for student use? It is not a secret weapon reserved just for teachers. Get as much use out of your lesson plans as is possible.

Student evaluation.   This is a topic by itself but is closely related to the lesson plan. If you are attempting to write performance type objectives for your lesson, then evaluation of students should be based upon stated objectives. Therefore, any test you construct or require students to take should be based upon the stated objectives that you list in your course of study and lesson plans. Do not list an objective unless you intend to measure the terminal performance outcome that results.

Why Use Lesson Plans?

The major argument for the use of lesson plans is to provide the best teacher-learning situation for students, and the plan should be one of the necessary items to help achieve the ideal situation.

The teacher who takes time and exerts effort in planning his teaching, considers many different items during his presentation phase. Some questions he might ask himself follow.

1. Is the material or demonstration of *sufficient importance* to present to the class as a group lesson? Perhaps it might be more suited to small group or individual instruction techniques.

2. Is the material or demonstration such that the best *method of presentation* is the lecture/demonstration technique? Perhaps, the material could be covered by a reading assignment, instruction sheet, video-tape, film, single-concept film, or some other form of educational technology.

3. Is the focus of the plan on the *main thing* to be learned by the students? Are the objectives of the lesson stated in a clear and concise form so that the main focus of the plan is clear?

4. Is the lesson content of such an *amount* that it can be presented within the normal interest span of the students? Normal interest span of individuals varies. After a few lessons most instructors can determine how long they will have the attention of their students.

5. Is the lesson content appropriate to the learners and their *past experiences*? Does the lesson in question relate to the previous experiences of the students, or is it completely unrelated?

6. Is the lesson plan structure such that it proceeds from the *known to the unknown*?

7. Is the lesson plan structure such that it proceeds from the *most simple to the most complex*?

8. Is the lesson plan structure such that the *outcome is measurable*? If you have attempted to base your instruction on performance objectives, then the outcome should be measurable.

Various Types of Lessons

Instructional strategy on the part of the teacher is a necessary part of his "bag of tricks." We all tend to get tired of hearing and seeing the same technique used day in and day out. Place yourself in the place of the students sometime. Better yet, have someone video-tape you and play back the tape to evaluate yourself. Chapter seven deals with a number of techniques to individualize instruction in the shop or laboratory setting and presents a variety of instructional strategies.

In dealing with shop classes of fifteen to twenty-five students, it is commonly necessary to make use of many formal lesson presentations. The entire subject of lesson plan construction to this point has been concerned with formal type lesson presentations. Most formal lessons presented by shop teachers fall into two basic types, the demonstration lesson and the theory lesson.

The demonstration lesson is a lesson planned for the learning of some skill involving active demonstrable performance on the part of the teacher as well as the students. Such lessons as the following would be demonstration types.

> Proper Use of the Cross-Cut Saw
> Adjusting the Breaker Points in an Automobile
> Hair Coloring
> Giving Injections

The theory type lesson is one planned for the learning of information or principles needed in the practice of a trade. Such lessons as the following would be theory types.

> Nail Sizes
> Theory of Internal Combustion
> Diseases of the Heart
> Parts of the Human Body

The important thing is not whether a lesson is a demonstration or related lesson, but the instructional strategy used to present the lesson. The lesson plan format suggested in this chapter is suitable to either type of lesson.

Lesson Plan Construction

The lesson plan form outlined in Figure 7–2 is suggested as a format for your own plans. The format is related to the structure suggested for the individual instructional units presented in Figure 6–1. The suggested lesson plan format is suitable for demonstration and theory type lessons.

Lesson Plan

TITLE

INTRODUCTORY STATEMENT

The actual introductory statement that will be used to introduce the lesson to the students.

BEHAVIORAL OBJECTIVES

The desired behavior of the students after the completion of the lesson or after application of the principles or skills. Skills that the students should be able to satisfactorily demonstrate in order to meet the stated objectives.

REFERENCES

A brief listing of the reference source or sources which students can consult for additional material on the subject.

INSTRUCTIONAL AIDS

A listing of the aids that are essential for the lesson. Hand tools, machine parts, measurement devices, films, slides, charts and anything else that you may need during the lesson.

THE PRESENTATION (INSTRUCTIONAL CONTENT)

Outline in sufficient detail of the instructional content to be included in the lesson. It will be from this outline that you will present the lesson. The arrangement should be such that the material is arranged starting with the most simple and proceeding to the most complex.

DISCUSSION — QUESTIONS

At the completion of the lesson, ask if the students have any questions. If not, have a series of your own questions to ask of them to determine their understanding of the material just presented.

APPLICATION

Assignment or practical work which will allow the students sufficient practice to master what is expected of them, in the stated lesson objectives.

EVALUATION CRITERIA

How the students will be evaluated. Should be based entirely on the stated behavioral objectives. This evaluation may take a number of forms including pencil and paper tests and/or performance tests.

FIGURE 7–2

Example Outline of a Lesson Plan

Further elaboration of each of the items suggested for inclusion in lesson plans follows.

Introductory statement. This should be the statement that you will use to introduce the lesson to the students. Think of yourself as a salesman selling your product, which is the lesson. If the lesson content is important enough to be a lesson, then tell the students so, as well as why. You might review what preceded and what will follow the lesson.

Behavioral objectives. A great deal has already been said about behavioral objectives in chapter three which was concerned with the development of a course of study. It takes time to write behavioral objectives, but the results should be worth the effort. As you no doubt, are aware, a well written behavioral objective will tell the student what is expected of him some time in the future. The future might be immediately after the lesson, in one week, one month, or at the end of the school year, but whatever the time, the knowledge or skill gained is the result of the lesson being taught. The objective will also indicate the conditions under which the student would be expected to perform and to what level of accuracy. A few examples of behavioral objectives associated with lesson presentations follows.

1. The student, given a Weston Model 611 tube tester, should be able to test and indicate the condition of a conventional vacuum tube within _____ minutes and do it successfully _____ percent of the time.
2. The student, given a rough draft of a one page business letter (one hundred words in body), should be able to type it with perfect accuracy within _____ minutes.
3. The student, shown fifteen different woodworking tools, should be able to identify _____ percent of them within _____ minutes.

The examples all have a number of things in common. Each describes some *action* (action verb) on the part of the student, and each has some *time* allotment involved in the statement. (Although it is possible you might not want to be concerned with time in some of your objectives.) Each has some *criterion measure* of level of performance, such as the percentage of the time that the student should be correct.

In the examples, the time and percent were purposely left blank. These two measures are determined by the teacher's knowledge of the students' levels. It is plausible to establish one criterion level of performance for the students one week after the lesson and another performance level for their final evaluation. As students gain more experience through doing, you could establish higher criterion levels. You would do this making sure that the students were fully aware of the situation and your reasons.

References.   References should remind you of the various sources (books, etc.) that you used in developing the lesson plan. It is a good idea to tell the students about the reference source so that they too, can go to it for additional and/or review information. In the event a substitute teacher was required to work from your lesson plan, he would know where to look for additional information.

Instructional aids.   In this section of the lesson plan, you should list *everything* you plan to use during the lesson. If you are giving a lesson on driving nails into lumber, make sure you list the hammer, nail, and lumber.

You should also list audiovisual devices that you plan to use, including the title and source of films and filmstrips. If you plan to give students an instruction sheet, indicate it and attach a copy to the lesson plan.

The presentation.   This is the major section of the lesson plan that you will be working from on the day of your lesson presentation. It should be an outline, in sufficient detail, of the instructional content to be included in the lesson. The outline should be such as to proceed from the simple to the complex. The procedure could be a list of teaching points arranged from number one on. Remember, it is mainly for your use and perhaps, at unexpected times, the use of a substitute teacher who we assume, has a similar background.

Think through or make a "dry run" of your lesson to check on the instructional procedure. Pick out the key points, always remembering that safety is perhaps the most important item.

Discussion — questions.   At the completion of your formal presentation, allow time for, and encourage, class discussion or questions from students regarding the lesson. Always include a few pertinent questions, so that if the class does not interact, you might be able to encourage the discussion through your questions.

Application.   Now that the lesson has been presented, do not just leave it without first telling the students how you expect them to apply it in the shop or laboratory. Most demonstration type lessons will involve practical application immediately on the part of the students.

Evaluation criteria.   Tell the students how they will be evaluated on the basis of the material just presented. The evaluation should be based entirely on the stated objectives of your lesson. This evaluation might be in terms of demonstrated performance on a "live job," a project, or a pencil and paper type test. The important item is to tell the students how they will be evaluated.

DISCUSSION QUESTIONS

1. Discuss the strong and weak points of the lesson plan format suggested in Figure 7–1.

2. Discuss the strong and weak points of the lesson plan format suggested in Figure 7–2.

3. Divide the members of the class into a number of small groups. Ask each group to write five behavioral objectives in one of the areas typically found in a vocational-technical school.

4. Discuss the procedures used in schools regarding lesson plan construction and operating procedures.

ASSIGNMENTS

1. Using the format suggested in Figure 7–2, prepare a demonstration type lesson plan. It should be designed for a _____ minute presentation.

2. Write ten behavioral objectives for your instructional specialization. These should be short-range objectives, not course objectives.

3. Find one of your old lesson plans and compare it to the one you prepared for assignment 1.

ADDITIONAL REFERENCES

Balassi, Sylvester J., *Focus on Teaching*. New York: The Odyssey Press, 1968.

Mager, Robert F., *Developing Attitude Toward Learning*. Palo Alto, California: Fearon Publishers, Inc., 1968.

Means, Richard K., *Methodology in Education*. Columbus, Ohio: Charles E. Merrill Publishing Company, 1968.

Proctor, James O. and G. Edward Griefzue, *TNT — Techniques, Notes, Tips for Teachers*. Albany, New York: Delmar Publishers, Inc., 1949.

Skinner, B. F., *The Technology of Teaching*. New York: Appleton-Century-Crofts, 1968.

U.S. Department of Health, Education and Welfare, *The Preparation of Occupational Instructors*. Washington, D.C.: U.S. Government Printing Office, 1966.

Part III   PRESENTATION

Chapter 8 THE FIRST DAY OF CLASS

The first day of a new school year can be a very trying day for the ill-prepared teacher. If advanced planning was well done, the day will be more bearable. Any number of first-day problems can occur through no fault of the teacher. Students can be somewhat confused if they are in a new school for the first time, and there are usually some scheduling problems. If the advanced planning suggested in the first three chapters was followed by the new teacher, the first day should be easier.

Each year many trade and industrial education teachers enter classrooms for the first time. These men and women enter the profession on the basis of industrial experiences in the trades and industry, and many lack courses beyond high school. When they enter teaching, they usually are required by local or state certification to take so many hours of credits toward a teaching certificate. It is a real change for the trades-teacher to be a craftsman one day and on the next, a teacher. In such a transition, the individual must be well prepared to meet the students.

School Procedure

Most schools offer a two or three-day orientation session for new staff members. At this time the school schedule and the general procedure to be followed by both students and teachers is explained. Forms and paper work usually required on the first day will also be covered during the orientation session. This is also a good opportunity to get acquainted with your fellow teachers.

The first day of school in some districts may last only a few hours. Other districts might start with a half-day or full-day session. The important thing is to be well prepared for the time you must spend with your classes during the first day. If your school starts with a full-day session, you may have your shop or laboratory students for as long as two or three hours which can be a long time for the teacher who is prepared to work with his class for only fifteen or twenty minutes. It is best to be over-prepared rather than under-prepared. It is generally the unprepared teacher who runs into discipline problems with his students. If students are kept busy in meaningful shop work, few problems will occur.

First day procedures vary from district to district. The following are some items of concern to the shop teacher.

1. Check your attendance list and make sure all are in your classroom. Report those whose names appear, but who are not present.
2. Complete any forms that are required by the local administration. You may want to use some form of data sheet for your own shop use. If so, have the students complete it. (If students are making out forms, make sure they understand the directions.)
3. Locks and lockers may be issued and assigned on the first day of class. Follow directions from the administration as to correct procedure and location of lockers.
4. Textbooks may be issued (loaned) to students on the first day. Note procedure and records to be used in issuing textbooks.

The four items listed above are in no way complete, but are given as an illustration of some of the things that might be necessary on the first day of school. You will have to look over your local school district's procedure for the opening of school for full particulars.

Be Over Prepared

It is much better to be over-prepared than underprepared when you meet your classes. To say the least, it is rather embarrassing to complete the lesson or demonstration for the students and find that you still have a half-hour or more remaining before the end of the period. This is an especially bad situation early in the school year when the students are not ready to work on their shop projects or assigned jobs.

The wise instructor will always be over-prepared and ready to go on with new material or review old material so that wasted time will be avoided. An instructor, in planning his lessons, should include questions, assignments, and practical applications of the lesson material. These items, in addition to being of instructional value, will serve to avoid wasted time in the shop or laboratory.

If the students are interested and the instructor is well prepared, there should be little wasted time. Remember too that busy students engaged in a meaningful learning experience are not going to cause discipline problems.

Discipline

A smoothly operating school is the responsibility of the administration, teachers, and students. All must work together in making the instructional setting as interesting as possible and one that operates with as few problems as possible. One weak link in the chain can cause all sorts of problems. The one weak link, be it an administrator, teacher or student, must be dealt with in a firm, fair, and consistent manner.

The beginning teacher should be familiar with his school's policy on discipline and the treatment of discipline cases. It is not possible to write case studies and ask new teachers how they would handle a particular situation and use it as a meaningful learning experience because problems of misconduct are so varied. One never knows when a problem will arise, and it is almost impossible to be prepared in advance to deal with all situations. When classroom problems do arise, attempt to stay cool and act in a firm, fair and, consistent manner. This is easier to say than do, but remember your students are human beings and expect to be treated in a fair manner. It could be that you, the teacher, may be the cause of some of the problems that exist. Did you get up on the wrong side of the bed this morning? Did you have an argument with your wife or husband at breakfast? Did you stay out too late last night? Are you in a bad mood? Are you poorly prepared for the day's lesson? It could be that students may have personal problems that affect their school behavior, so there are a multitude of possibilities that can cause things to go wrong.

When a problem does occur, attempt to stay cool, and think before you act. Do not run hot and cold from one day to the next.

Many beginning teachers are asked to leave a teaching position because of their inability to maintain discipline. It is good advice to a beginning teacher to start off as a strong disciplinarian and then ease off as the year goes on. It is the teacher who starts off the year as a weak disciplinarian and then attempts to tighten up control who runs into difficulties.

Try to handle your own discipline cases. Do not rely upon the assistant principal or principal to handle your problems. Only in the most serious cases, should you make use of administrative help. Of course, you should seek the advice of your administrators and experienced fellow teachers, but handle your own discipline cases as they arise. Both your students and administrators will respect you for handling your own classroom problems. The teacher who is continually sending students to the office for discipline is developing a reputation both with the office staff and the students.

The main purpose of effective control or discipline in a classroom or shop is to permit the most effective use of instructional time. This does not mean that military control and order is necessary in the school. Control that is conducive to good learning is what is desired.

A few suggestions worthy of your consideration follow:

1. Act in a firm, fair, and consistent manner when handling discipline cases.
2. Do not make snap judgements or decisions in handling discipline cases. Think before you act.
3. Never act when you are angry. Cool off; consider the situation and act only when you are fully composed.
4. Never make fun of, or humiliate, a student. Students are human beings and should be treated as such.
5. Never use corporal punishment in handling a discipline case. Such a serious case should be handled by the administration.
6. Do not punish an entire class in order to discipline one or two students.
7. Being well prepared is one technique used in avoiding problems. It is during periods of wasted instructional time that most problems will occur.
8. Establish a definite classroom procedure when pupils enter and leave the classroom.
9. Be consistent. Use disciplinary action suitable to the offense.
10. Handle discipline cases in private and not in front of the class. But make sure that the other students are aware that the situation will be dealt with.

Student Records

It would be a good idea to review the school records of your students before the first day of class. The records would provide you with some background information about your students and their past level of achievement. In order to avoid an improper interpretation of the information, it would be to your advantage to ask the counselor to look over the records with you.

School policies vary, so do not be shocked if the records are not made available to you. But at least, find out if they can be made available to you.

Introduction of Self and Students

If you are meeting the students in your class for the first time, introduce yourself and relate the highlights and industrial experiences that you have had in the past. Also, ask each student to introduce himself or herself and say something about their past education and work experiences.

This procedure will sort of set the stage for the year and should be of value to both the students and the teacher.

First Impressions

The students will be gaining their first impression of you and likewise, you of them. No matter what you might have heard about a student (or students) in your class, make it clear to them that they are starting the year with a "clean record." You will form your impression of each student as the school year moves on. Make this clear to the students the first day of class. First impressions are important, but the impressions based on a term or two are much more valid.

Introduction of Course and Objectives

It is important that you introduce the course and its stated objectives to your students on the first day of class. In a sense, you are selling the course to the student, but in another sense, you are informing them of what they can expect in the course. On the basis of your presentation, some students might decide they have made a wrong decision and do not want to take the course after all. Make provisions for them to see their counselor and arrange a transfer to some other program or specialization.

Inform all the students about the course and the long-range outcome expected of them. It is important that the class be as fully informed as possible about the course and its relationship to the total program. By the total program, is implied a three-year program in electronics. If you are teaching the first-year course in electronics, relate the course to the total three-year program. In other words, relate the course you are teaching to the total school program for the year and the long-range program leading to graduation.

It is desirable to be teaching from a course of study, and the stated objectives should be included in the course of study. Chapter five dealt with the course of study in much more detail, as well as with the writing of behavioral objectives.

Relate the stated objectives of the course to the students so that they are aware of the desired outcomes which will be expected of them at the end of the course. It is to the student's advantage if the objectives are stated in behavioral terms. A few examples follow.

Electronics

The student given a properly functioning radio receiver, of the 8-transistor type, must be able to *take* and *record* the proper voltage readings within fifteen minutes.

The student given the necessary parts to make a power supply must be able to *assemble, wire,* and *solder* them within a one-hour time period.

The student must be able to correctly *solve* at least five simple Ohms law problems within twenty-five minutes.

Drafting

Given an object (model, tool, etc.), the student must be able to correctly *draw* an assembly drawing of it within a two-hour period of time.

Hairstyling

Given an illustration (photo) the student must be able to *style* the model's hair in a similar manner within forty-five minutes.

It is possible to state your instructional objectives in behavioral terms. The key is action verbs, with stated conditions and times. Students should be made aware that they will be evaluated in terms of the stated instructional objectives. This evaluation will occur during, and at the end of, the course.

Method of Student Evaluation

The method of student evaluation as stated above, should be based upon the stated instructional objectives. Just as the instructor informs the class of the instructional objectives of the course, he should tell the students how their final grade will be determined. Well written instructional objectives stated in behavioral terms will make it possible for students to assess their own progress to a very large extent.

All schools will have some sort of structured marking system for reporting student progress to parents. The shop teacher just as any other teacher in the school system will have to operate within the structure of the marking system. Let us use the following as an example: Smithville Vocational High School reports student grades to parents every ten weeks. There are four ten-week marking periods plus a final examination. The final grade is arrived at by averaging the four quarter grades and the final examination grade. Each grade counts 20 percent toward the final grade.

TABLE 8–1

Numerical Grading System

10 weeks	20 weeks	30 weeks	40 weeks	Final Exam	Final Grade
80	85	75	90	75	81

$$80 + 85 + 75 + 90 + 75 = 405 \div 5 = 81$$

As seen in Table 8–1, the final grade of 81 resulted from the average of the four quarters and the final examination grade.

Though the teacher must operate within the marking system used in the school, he is responsible for arriving at the grades to be reported each quarter. It is this information that should be conveyed to the students during the first day of class. Will you base the quarter grades on shop work, pencil and paper tests, or assignments? How will you record grades in your classbook?

Students should be informed about the school's marking system and how it is operated. The students should also be informed by the teacher as to how their quarter grades will be arrived at. Pupil-teacher planning can be used by the teacher to arrive at a fair system of student evaluation. Evaluation, if it is to be effective, should not be kept secret from the students. After all, it is the students who are being rated.

Part four will also address itself to evaluation. It will include class records, test construction, and evaluation and should help you in evaluation of student performance.

Student Requirements — Quality and Quantity

Closely associated with student evaluation is the topic of student requirements and the quality of workmanship expected of the students. Again, it would be wise to repeat that well written instructional objectives stated in behavioral terms will indicate to the students the level of performance expected of them.

The students should be informed as to what the course requirements are and what level of craftsmanship is expected of them for successful completion of the course. The experienced teacher would do it in such a way as to arouse student interest in the project or activities that the class will be involved in.

The requirements should not be presented in such a way as to make them seem as a barrier to successful course completion. This will only scare off some students and shock others, which is not the purpose of reviewing course requirements.

The experienced teacher would do little more than relate the experiences, activities, jobs, projects, and assignments that the students must master before the end of the course. He is relating to the students the level of achievement and craftsmanship expected of them by the end of the course. It should be a positive, rather than negative approach.

Examples of the work, projects, and achievements of former students should be shown and/or related to the class. A former graduate or student might be asked to come in and relate his experiences to the new students.

Shop Tour

If it is the first time the students have been in the shop, it would be a good idea to conduct a tour of the shop. During the tour, the instructor would point out the various features, machines, and areas of the shop to the students. Special consideration should be given to safety zones and the other safety features that exist in the shop. The tour should be more than a quick walk through the shop. Questions should be encouraged from the students. It should be obvious that advanced preparation of the shop was carried out by the instructor. It would be foolish to take the students on a tour of a messy shop facility.

Safety Instruction

Safety regulations and procedures were discussed in detail in chapter three. Safety instruction is included in this chapter only to remind the teacher that safety instruction should begin the first day of class and continue each and every day of the school year.

The instructor will have to decide how much time to spend on safety instruction the first day. At least some mention of safety should be made.

A review of the shop safety regulations should be conducted as early as possible in the school year.

Daily Procedure

The students should be informed about what the daily procedure will be in the shop. This procedure can, and no doubt will, vary from shop to shop and teacher to teacher. When the students enter, should they be seated, change to work clothes, or go to work? Explain what procedure you want the students to follow. One example follows.

1. When you enter the shop, sit in your assigned seat.
2. Attendance will be taken. Announcements will be made. A lesson, if scheduled, will be presented.
3. Change to suitable shop dress. (Optional depending upon specialization.)
4. Carry on with shop assignment, project, or work as required.
5. When the clean-up signal is given, stop work, replace tools, and do your assigned job.
6. When your clean-up assignment is completed, change from work clothes and return to your assigned seat.
7. Wait until dismissed by the instructor. (The bell is not for students, it is for the instructor.)

The above is just an example. You should decide on a procedure and make sure that it is followed by the students. A set procedure will save you many problems and result in a smoother operation of the shop.

DISCUSSION QUESTIONS

1. Divide the class into groups of three to five students by specialization. (Automotive instructors in one group, cosmetology teachers in another, etc.) Each group should discuss a list of objectives for their particular specialization.

2. Invite a first-year vocational teacher to be a guest speaker in the class. Ask the first-year teacher to discuss his or her experiences based on the first day of classes. The discussion should then be expanded to include the teacher's experiences from the total first year.

ASSIGNMENTS

1. Outline the daily procedure that you plan to use in your shop.

2. List the objectives, as you see them, of the specialization you are prepared to teach.

3. Outline the method of student evaluation that you plan to use, which would be workable within the structure of the school's formal grading system.

ADDITIONAL REFERENCES

Doros, Sidney, *Teaching as a Profession*. Columbus, Ohio: Charles E. Merrill Publishing Company, 1968.

Hicks, William U. and Frank H. Blackington, *Introduction to Education*. Columbus, Ohio: Charles E. Merrill Publishing Company, 1965.

McKean, Robert C., *Principles and Methods in Secondary Education*. Columbus, Ohio: Charles E. Merrill Publishing Company, 1962.

Oliva, Peter F. and Ralph A. Scrafford, *Teaching in a Modern Secondary School*. Columbus, Ohio: Charles E. Merrill Publishing Company, 1965.

Proctor, James O. and G. Edward Griefzu, *TNT — Techniques, Notes, Tips for Teachers*. Albany, New York: Delmar Publishers, Inc., 1949.

Skinner, B. F., *The Technology of Teaching*. New York: Appleton-Century-Crofts, 1968.

Trow, William Clark, *Teacher and Technology: New Designs for Learning*. New York: Appleton-Century-Crofts, 1963.

Chapter 9　THE TEACHING-LEARNING SITUATION

Most of the formal educational process takes place in the school. Learning, of course, takes place both in and out of school. The major concern of this book is the formal learning situation that exists or should exist in our shops and laboratories. This is referred to as the *teaching-learning situation*. It is the responsibility of both the teacher and the student to make the teaching-learning situation the best possible with the given physical conditions.

The intent of this chapter is not to review learning theory as that subject can be best covered in books dealing with the way people learn. The intent is to describe some of the factors that might influence the teaching-learning situation and your possible success or failure as a teacher.

Definition

Courses of study, instructional strategy, instructional materials and lesson plans all help contribute to the development of a sound teaching-learning situation. The formal learning situations that exist under the control of the school can be considered teaching-learning situations. These situations would include both in-

111

school and out-of-school programs such as cooperative type educational programs. A cooperative type program is one in which the student attends class for a half-day and then is placed with a cooperating employer for three or more hours of on-the-job type training.

Certain items are essential to the systematic development of the teaching-learning situation. The burden of responsibility rests with the teacher in establishing the climate for the teaching-learning situation. The active involvement of the learner in developing the teaching-learning situation has already been discussed in earlier pages. Figure 9–1 diagrams the suggested procedure to be followed in establishing the teaching-learning situation. The theme of this book is aimed at the development of the teaching-learning situation based on the developmental procedure suggested in Figure 9–1. The entire procedure should always be involved in a continual evaluation process with the goal being to provide the best teaching-learning process.

Pressures on the School

To some extent the teaching-learning situation, is influenced by the pressures which are brought to bear on the total school system. Some of these influences are reflected in school board policy and the amount of funds available for the instructional process. All school systems face the constant pressures and influences of the tax supported structure of the system. Additional pressures are exercised by the various boards of education which must determine policy for the school system. Active parent groups can also influence the direction of the school program. In recent years, we have seen student activism demonstrated on both our college campuses and at the secondary level. All of these factors influence or exert pressure on the system and, in turn, on the teaching-learning situation which is the major responsibility of the teacher.

Vocational education programs by their very nature stand accountable for supplying trained manpower to the industrial community. The success or failure of the vocational program to meet this need is always under evaluation by the employers within the community.

The world of work has a very strong influence on the educational program of any vocational education program. Those individuals responsible for the vocational education program must be well acquainted with the industrial developments that are and will be occurring. They must be concerned with the technological advances of industry and the needs of industry as related to employment requirements (skills) and employee needs. Industrial leaders should be asked to become advisors in vocational education program planning and evaluation.

DEVELOPING TEACHING-LEARNING SITUATIONS

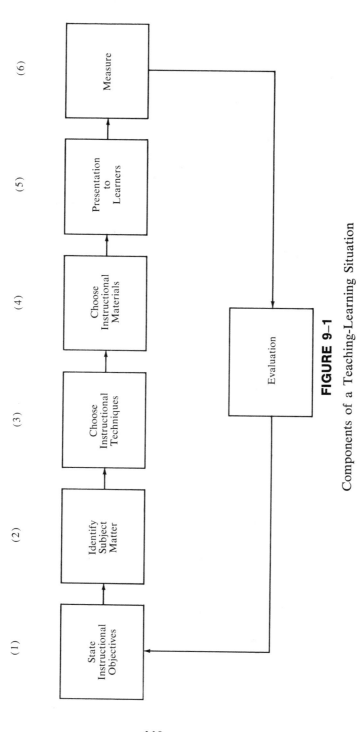

FIGURE 9–1

Components of a Teaching-Learning Situation

Well spelled out performance objectives will help the industrial community know what your graduates are capable of doing and to what level of expertise they can expect them to measure up. The active participation of your curriculum advisory committee will assure some level of understanding between the school and the industrial community.

You will note some of these pressures more than others. The important thing is to get on with the job and provide the best teaching-learning situation that you are able to provide under the given conditions.

Making the Program Relevant

A common word among educators and students at the present time is the word relevant. The students' plea is that the school program be relevant to the society that exists outside the bricks and mortar of the school building. Educators use the word relevant in speeches and in articles for publication. Both teachers and students are concerned about how relevant the school curriculum is to the problems and conditions that exist outside of the school. If vocational education programs are not relevant to the industrial employment needs of the community, state, and country, a low rate of job placement should be noted in follow-up studies of past vocational graduates. However, one must use care in evaluating the success or failure of vocational high school graduates on the basis of job placement alone. In times of a scarce supply of skilled manpower, the poorly trained and educated may very well be able to obtain jobs. In times of a plentiful supply of manpower, skilled jobs will go to those individuals best prepared for specialized occupations.

As a vocational educator, it would be to your advantage to keep as up-to-date in your specialization as possible. Then you should attempt to incorporate the latest industrial advances into your course of study.

It would be to your students' advantage as well as yours if you would contact the various employers of your graduates in order to attempt to determine their strengths and weaknesses. This feedback information should prove helpful in making modifications in your course of study. This technique plus the active involvement of a curriculum advisory committee should help you keep your program relevant to the needs of students.

A relevant education program involves more than just the skills and knowledges essential for employment. The total educational program should prepare students for life. With the rapid changes in technology occurring, it may very well be necessary for an individual to change his employment and specialization a number of times during his life span. Educators should build into the curriculum the necessary and essential elements of study needed for life. This, of course, would include those skills essential for a vocation as one of the ingredients necessary for life skills.

As a vocational educator, you are in a unique position to provide a really meaningful and relevant program for your students. In order to do this, you must be willing to keep up-to-date with the advances in your specialization and the skills necessary to master them. A vocational educator should be a unique individual who is able to "make it" as a teacher in the public school system or as a skilled craftsman in his specialization. Try not to find yourself out-dated in your specialization after five years as a shop or laboratory teacher. The basic success or failure rests with the teachers who are on the firing line in the shops and laboratories of the vocational-technical schools in this country.

The Teacher — His Role

The teacher is the subject matter expert in the teaching-learning situation. The subject may be English, social studies, mathematics, machine design, or cosmetology. The teacher is a part of the situation since he has the necessary expertise, including both theory and practical experience, to render instruction and assistance to learners. The teacher is responsible for keeping up-to-date with advances in his subject field as well as in educational theory. The teacher is responsible for setting the teaching-learning situation into operation and keeping it moving from the most simple to the most complex material to be covered in the course. The instructional content is the responsibility of the teacher. Well stated course objectives are essential in order to keep the level of the course up to where it should be.

When the door to the shop or classroom closes, it is the teacher who leads the way in establishing the climate for the teaching-learning situation. Traditional type teachers will stick to traditional methods and techniques. Innovative teachers will experiment and always seek new and exciting techniques to improve the teacher-learning situation. It is at this point that the stage is set and that students either become actively involved in the process or become passive to the situation. The question is, "Which will you be?"

The Student

Some have said that the teaching profession would be great if it were not for the students. No doubt, this statement has been said in fun with no serious intent. We must always remember that students come to school as consumers of what the school has to offer.

They leave for the world of work as the products of the school. If students had their choice of schools and teachers, just like we have our choice of physicians, dentists, lawyers, skilled tradesmen, and many other specialists, many classrooms and schools might be empty.

All educational personnel must be willing to stand accountable for the program they are providing the students. Accountability does not just rest with the superintendent or principal, as it is the responsibility of each and every staff member in the school. In preparing for your assignment and lessons, never lose sight of the fact that you are in the shop or laboratory to provide a service to the consumers, the students. Many self-centered individuals lose sight of this factor and feel they are providing a great service to education by their very presence in the school. It is at this point that it is easy for a teacher to turn bitter and almost hate students.

STUDENT NEEDS

The teacher must assume that students are in his shop or laboratory because they want to be. It must be pointed out that in many cases this assumption is not 100 percent correct. However, the teacher must assume that students enter his shop or laboratory because they want to take part in the teaching-learning situation that exists there. The "good" teacher can take full advantage of such a situation and get on with the job. The "poor" teacher will destroy a good situation, lose students or become so discouraged that he might leave his teaching position.

Students are human just like yourself and should be treated with the respect and dignity with which you expect others to treat you. No two students will be exactly alike. Each student will have his own problems, ambitions, and bad days just like everyone else, including teachers.

Students need to be accepted by fellow students and the teacher. Call students by name and show an interest in each one, both as a learner and as an individual. Encourage small group work as the opportunities exist in planning your instructional strategy. The instructional setting should duplicate as closely as possible the situation the students will later face in industry as employees. This involves both the social and the technological climates that would exist in the industrial setting.

Students need to have a sense of security. The development of the teaching-learning situation should be such as to make the student feel he has a place in the situation. He must feel a part of the setting and be secure in the situation. When students have done a good job, tell them that you are pleased with their progress. Provide opportunities for your students to discuss items of concern to them in private with you. See to it that the physical and instructional climates are as good as you can make them.

Students need to have approval by others. Encourage the most advanced student to do even better work. Let him know his work is very good and that he is making excellent progress. Encourage the slower students and when they make advances let them know that you are pleased. The teaching-learning situation should be geared to success and not failure. Many educators talk about a "zero-reject" system in which even the slowest student is not destined to failure. You will control the situation that exists in your shop or laboratory and whether it is geared to success or failure.

Many students like to help others. Advanced students may be asked to help some of the slower students in the shop. Encourage group projects and assignments as a means of encouraging group interaction and a sharing of learning experiences.

Students must be constantly reminded that they are preparing for employment when they leave the vocational program. Their employment success and level of salary to a large extent, will depend upon the level of skill they are able to develop in the vocational program. Employment security and economic independence should be one of the major needs of your students. Likewise, your skills and planning will help the students achieve employment security after they graduate.

THE STUDENT'S ROLE

The student, as is implied in the word, is in the role of the learner in the teaching-learning situation. Teachers should view students as consumers or customers in the educational setting. The student is attending the school to prepare for his future, which might involve still more formal education or immediate employment after leaving.

In the teaching-learning situation, the instructional strategy and course content depend mainly on the teacher. The students should enter and be a part of the teaching-learning situation with the idea to get as much out of the experience as possible. Many students, if conditioned properly, by past educational experiences, will attempt to get the very most out of the teaching-learning situation. Other students will play a much less active role. The expert teacher will attempt to draw them out and get them involved in the shop and laboratory activities that are under way.

If the teacher has laid the stage properly, students will be made to feel a very active part in the teaching-learning situation. Much will depend upon their past educational experiences and contacts with other teachers. Many students, due to the nature of the educational system, are apt to place themselves in a passive role within the teaching-learning situation. It will be difficult for students of this type to adjust to the new found freedom of being in a teaching-learning situation where the learner is expected to be an active participant.

The student should feel comfortable in the teaching-learning situation. The student needs to have a sense of security and belonging within the educational setting. It is the teacher's responsibility to develop the setting and make the students' feel a part of the action. This does not mean a free-wheeling, do-nothing atmosphere should exist in the shop or laboratory. The educational process is still under way and active involvement is encouraged to facilitate the teaching-learning situation.

Students should realize the importance of getting as much practical experience as possible during their limited stay in school. They must be made to realize that schooling is preparation for life, and the skills and knowledges essential for entering the world of work are an important function of the teaching-learning situation.

Just as the teacher has responsibilities in deciding upon the instructional strategy and content, the student has responsibilities in learning the content and mastering the skills involved. Well stated behavioral objectives will assist both teacher and student in knowing what is expected of both.

INDIVIDUAL DIFFERENCES

We all should realize that no two people are alike. There is only one you with your strengths and weaknesss. No two students in your class will be identical in aptitude, ability, and behavior characteristics.

Each time you plan for a new school term or for an individual lesson, try and remember that all the students with whom you will use the lesson plan are different. In a class of fifteen, it would be best no doubt, time permitting, to prepare fifteen lesson plans, one for each student. Planning time of course does not permit this type of preparation, so we manage with one plan. Teachers who attempt to master the technique of individual instruction are concerned with a custom-tailored instructional program for each student in the class. More will be said about individualization of instruction in chapter eleven.

Just as physical characteristics of individuals vary to a large extent, so do the non-physical characteristics. No one would ask the ninety-pound weakling in a class to carry a heavy object any great distance. Yet, we may very well be expecting great things from a student with limited mental ability. The point is to be aware of the non-physical characteristics of our students.

Attempt to gather as much information about your students as is available. Such information is usually obtained from the guidance counselors in the school. Some items of concern would be as follows:

A. Any special physical disability that might delimit a student's career

B. Past academic achievement in school

C.   Reading grade level based on standardized tests
D.   Mathematics grade level based on standardized tests
E.   IQ scores (subject to limitations)

Each of the indicated items are best explained by a properly prepared guidance counselor who can interpret the IQ scores and scores on standardized tests.

When students enter your class for the first time, let them know you will form your opinion of them on the basis of their involvement and behavior in your class. Anything that might have happened in past years and with other teachers is not of concern to you. Each student should start with a clean record in your class. If you look for a problem from a particular student, you will probably create one.

A good teacher will attempt to observe and understand each student in his class. The teacher should believe in the dignity of the individual and attempt to treat each student as he himself likes to be treated.

Course work in educational psychology, learning theory, and vocational guidance will all help to improve one's understanding of individual differences. Always remember that you are teaching students. The subject matter, be it baking or sewing, is the content and stands second after your primary influence on students. Attempt to relate to your students and get to know them as individuals within the class setting.

Treatment of Students

Students can have bad days just as teachers often have days when things do not go just according to schedule. Many students come to school each day with personal problems that are not known to the teacher. Illness, family problems, other influencing factors often plague students just as they do teachers. The experienced, student-orientated teacher will develop a sense of understanding for the problems that at times influence student behavior.

No one likes a person who acts one way one time and another way at another time, given the same conditions. It is difficult to work for a boss who runs hot and cold under the same given conditions, depending upon his mood. As you move through your first years of teaching, you will in a sense, be establishing your own procedures. Consistent treatment of students should be an essential ingredient of your policies. A treatment that varies from day to day will gain little respect for the teacher from his students.

Many times teachers have to make decisions under trying classroom conditions involving student behavior. Be cautious of making snap judgements that influence other people. If you lose your temper, attempt to "cool off" before making a decision that you may regret later. Do not be afraid to admit an incorrect decision and attempt to correct the situation. Teachers are human and have all the weaknesses of any human.

What technique works for one teacher might not work for another. It is difficult to be a role player and act differently than you normally do.

Attempt to be *firm, fair,* and *consistent* in the treatment of students. The first few days with any new class are essentially the most important of the year as they set the stage for what is to follow. It is much better to be too strict early in the year as you can always ease off. If you start and fail to exercise good control, it is very difficult to regain it as the year goes on. It is essential that the teacher establish some ground rules as to the procedure necessary for the operation of the shop or laboratory. Such beginning ground rules should be subject to change as the conditions dictate.

Teaching is not a popularity contest. Do not be concerned about being the good guy and the buddy of your students. You can lose the respect of the students if you put yourself on their level. You are the teacher, a paid professional, and they are the students. The relationship between the teacher and students should be kept at a professional level in the class-room situation. Many good guy, buddy type teachers do not survive the first year of their teaching careers. A friendly atmosphere should exist in the classroom, but one in which the student and teacher both know their respective roles.

As problems occur involving students, remember the three key words — *firm, fair, consistent* — and let them guide you in the situation at hand. You must be firm and let the student know you mean business in settling the situation. Be fair to all students and treat them alike. Do not deal out unreasonable punishments for minor violations. Be consistent in your treatment of students and in the rules and regulations that need to be enforced in the shop. Safety regulations are of special importance in the shop, and violations of them should be dealt with immediately.

Students will respect the teacher who plays by the rules and treats them with equal respect and fairness. They should realize that every minute of class time used by the teacher in playing policeman is multi-plied by the number of students in the class. In a class of fifteen, if the teacher is forced to discipline a student and such action takes five min-utes, it amounts to seventy-five minutes of wasted time for the total class. The shop teacher should always attempt to relate the shop atmosphere to the on-the-job atmosphere in industry. Time is valuable and means money to an employer. The goof-off will soon be among the unemployed.

DISCIPLINE

Attempt to handle all of your own discipline cases yourself. The teachers who continually send students to the office soon lose the respect of the administration as well as the students. Certain school policy violations, by regulation, might have to be reported to the office. Try to handle any problems within your shop or laboratory by yourself.

There will be times when you need to send a student to the person who handles discipline cases. Usually it is a good idea to accompany the student to the office, so that a full discussion of the situation can take place. However, a shop instructor should *never* leave his students unsupervised for even a second. If it is impossible to accompany the student to the office, call the office, if you have a phone in the shop. If you cannot call, give the student a note to take to the office, and as soon as you can, go to the office to follow-up on the situation. Check your local policy or building manual for the suggested procedure within your school.

To be meaningful, discipline must occur at the time of the violation or problem. It does little good to delay the discipline action for a day or week. If there is to be some form of punishment, it should be carried out as soon as possible. Again, make sure you review local school policy on discipline procedure before you find yourself in violation of school policy.

Discipline should be handled in a firm, fair, and consistent manner as was indicated earlier. If some form of punishment is dealt out, it should be consistent with the violation.

You must find your own system and techniques as a disciplinarian. It is one of the unpleasant tasks involved in being a teacher, but it is essential for the smooth operation of your class and the school. All teachers and students must work together to provide the best conditions for the teaching-learning situation.

HANDLING SPECIAL PROBLEMS

Use all the resources of the school to handle student-centered problems that you might be involved in. If you make note of a special problem that a student seems to have, it is usually best to speak to the student's guidance counselor about the particular student. Such problems might be physical, emotional, achievement centered, or personal in nature. The guidance counselor might have information available about the student, or if it seems necessary to have additional information and reports, can obtain the necessary information. Consultative services of professional psychologists, physicians, and social case workers can be made available. There is usually a clear school policy on the procedure to be used in requesting such special services. The procedure usually starts with the student's counselor.

Case studies of various student problems could be related. However, their value might be limited to the classroom teacher since in an entire teaching career a teacher might never experience a similar case. The best advice to the beginning teacher is to consult with the counselor of a student who you feel might have a special problem. The classroom teacher is just not prepared to be everything to every student. Make use of the various professionals that are usually available to serve the school system.

Overview

An attempt has been made in this chapter to review some items which should be relevant to the teaching-learning situation. Learning theory and educational psychology is essential to the beginning teacher, but such subjects are left to other courses within your teacher preparation program. How people learn is an essential ingredient to the development of an instructional strategy used by the teacher. Such principles are left to the educational psychologists.

DISCUSSION QUESTIONS

1. Discuss the six major areas in Figure 9–1, Developing Teaching-Learning Situations. List the essential elements in each of the six major areas in the figure.

2. Invite a guidance counselor from a local vocational school to be a guest in the class. Have the counselor explain his role in the total school program. What services can the counselor provide for students and teachers?

3. Each member of the class should review the policies of a school district in regard to discipline procedures within the district. Discuss the relative advantages and disadvantages of the various procedures.

ASSIGNMENTS

1. Prepare a written report on the procedures used to handle discipline cases. Such procedures should be taken from a school's policy or teacher's manual. This will give you an opportunity to review a policy of which you should be aware.

2. Review the school policy on referral of students with special problems. In other words, what role does the teacher have in referring students who might need professional-medical services not available in the school?

3. What can you do to make your course relevant to the needs of your students? How will you keep your course content up-to-date with modern industrial practices?

ADDITIONAL REFERENCES

Bruner, Jerome S., *Toward A Theory of Instruction.* New York: W.W. Norton & Company, Inc., 1966.

Clayton, Thomas E., *Teaching and Learning.* Englewood Cliffs, New Jersey: Prentice-Hall, Inc., 1965.

DeCecco, John P., *Human Learning in the School.* New York: Holt, Rinehart & Winston, Inc., 1963.

Means, Richard K., *Methodology in Education.* Columbus, Ohio: Charles E. Merrill Publishing Company, 1968.

Parker, J. Cecil and Louis J. Rubin, *Process as Content.* Chicago: Rand McNally & Co., 1966.

Skinner, B.F., *The Technology of Teaching.* New York: Appleton-Century-Crofts, 1968.

Chapter 10 THE LESSON PRESENTATION

This chapter focuses on the presentation of a formal lesson to a group of students. The formal lesson presentation is only one technique and may be used or not used depending upon the teaching style of the instructor. Most instructors will find it necessary to present formal lessons and demonstrations to the entire class at various times, even though most of the other instruction might be of an individualized nature. It is but one technique and should be used when suited to the needs of the students and teacher.

By this time you should have had the opportunity to develop a few sample lesson plans based upon the format for lesson plan construction suggested in chapter seven. Now you should have the opportunity to have a practice run of the lesson. If a video tape recorder is available, it would be a good idea to have someone video tape the presentation and then rerun it for your own self-evaluation. If this is not possible, it is suggested that you at least tape record the presentation and then listen to the tape. Video tape recording has proven a valuable experience for many teachers who have had the opportunity to present a lesson and then evaluate their own performance.

The Importance of the Presentation

Even with the best of lesson plans to work from, you have no guarantee of your ability to present the lesson to a group of students. However you will be much better off with a good lesson plan than without one when making the presentation. The pre-planning spent in developing the lesson plan should pay off in the presentation.

The presentation is important for a number of reasons.

1. The content of the lesson must be of such a priority and importance as to make it necessary for such a lesson in the first place.
2. The formal lesson presentation method (lecture, demonstration, related) is the best means to present the lesson content to the students. If individualized instruction or some other instructional strategy was suitable, it would be used rather than the formal presentation.
3. Since the presentation is essential, students must be aware of the need and what is to follow. The application of the lesson content to their practical situations must be made clear.
4. Timing the presentation is of high priority. Timing does not refer to the amount of minutes or hours necessary for the actual presentation. It refers to its proper place in the instructional process. The presentation should be applicable within a very short period of time. In simple language, the student should be able to apply the principles taught within a day or so of the presentation.
5. The teacher is on display to the entire class during a formal lesson presentation. His ability to present a lesson to the class but yet relate to each individual in the class is now being evaluated by each student. His preparation, teaching style, and technical subject matter ability are all on display to his students.
6. The presentation is time consuming to both teacher and learner. It is essential that instructional time not be wasted by either the teacher or the learner. A well prepared teacher and well prepared student will help guard against lost instructional time. It is essential to make good use of the instructional time spent in presenting the lesson.

Pre-Planning

The importance of pre-planning was discussed earlier in the chapter concerned with the construction of lesson plans. The time spent in preparing the course of study and the lesson plans should now all begin to pay off in the quality of the actual lesson presentation. Many rather embarrassing situations can be avoided by good pre-planning. The following could all have been avoided if sufficient pre-planning had taken place.

1. You prepared a lesson plan and estimated that it would take thirty minutes to make the presentation. The actual presentation time was fifteen minutes and left you unprepared for the remaining fifteen minutes. That extra time can be very long to the under prepared teacher.

2. You are in the middle of a demonstration lesson presentation and find that you are missing an essential part or tool. It is especially embarrassing if you cannot locate the part or tool in the shop.

3. You have started your presentation to the class and are now ready to use a filmstrip projector. You turn it on, and the bulb does not light. The well prepared instructor would have a spare bulb handy to replace the defective one.

4. You have started a demonstration type presentation and find it essential to use a mathematical formula before you can continue with the demonstration. In preparing for the presentation, you neglected to review the formula and find yourself unable to continue with the demonstration.

BE OVER PREPARED

It is much better to be over prepared for a presentation than under prepared. This does not imply that you would continue with the presentation beyond the normal time you usually spend in your lesson presentations. It means that you have built-in safeguards in the form of follow-up or review questions which should follow the presentation. Another safeguard would be to provide individual laboratory work so that the students could apply the material just presented. To be of the most value the presentation should be of immediate need and use to the students. A delay in application will probably require a re-teach or review of the presentation and result in wasted instructional time.

The beginning student teacher or in-service teacher is most apt to underestimate the time necessary to present a certain topic. For this reason, it is essential that he be over prepared and have back-up questions or an immediate application procedure for the students to follow.

SETTING THE STAGE

The teacher, lesson plans in hand, must set the physical stage for the actual presentation. The physical setting should be an important ingredient to be considered in the pre-planning for the presentation. A number of suggestions seem worthy of note at this time.

Physical Facility.   The location for the presentation should be the setting in the shop or laboratory most conducive to the teaching-learning situation. You should be concerned about the comfort of your students. At times, especially for demonstration type lessons, it is necessary for the students to stand in order to see a demonstration on certain machines or equipment. The students will usually be seated in an area of the shop for most of the presentations. Provide proper chairs for the students. It is very difficult for students to have to sit on benches during a lesson presentation and be expected to pay attention and take notes. Do not require the students to sit in an area in which you would not want to sit.

Use care in the selection of your position to present the lesson. Do not place yourself in front of a large window area or bright lights that would require students to look toward glaring sunlight or bright lights. Guard against outside distractions in selecting the instructional area. Outside distractions are of two types, those that exist outside the shop and can be seen through the windows, and those that may or may not be visible depending upon whether there are windows in the door or wall facing the corridor.

All instructors need to be aware of crowding especially during demonstrations on machines or live work. If a lesson is being presented on the lathe, it is essential that students stand back far enough so that everyone can see. The instructor must constantly be concerned with crowding and lack of visibility. Closed circuit television (CCTV) and video tape recording (VTR) equipment can help the instructor who is willing to use such equipment in the shop and laboratory. CCTV and VTR equipment should be especially helpful to shop and laboratory instructors in presenting demonstration lessons which are difficult to present to large groups of students. The thoughtful instructor will always be aware of and attempt to improve the instructional setting for the lessons.

Lighting-Heating-Ventilation.   Before the start of any lesson or in fact any activity in the shop, make sure that you have proper lighting, temperature control, and ventilation. Even on the coldest day, fresh air is essential where a large group of people are assembled. Temperature control is essential and should be maintained between seventy and seventy-two degrees Fahrenheit. Lighting should be suitable since it is controlled by building specifications of the various state departments of education. Ability to reduce artificial and natural lighting is also essential if visual aids such as movies, slides, single-concept films, etc., are to be used. Shades or blinds of one or more types should be available to shut off outside light, if darkening of the shop is to be accomplished.

Student Comfort.   Many of the items previously mentioned were concerned with student comfort. Student comfort does not imply that the shop or laboratory be a plush recreation area for various activities. The shop or laboratory must be similar to the conditions that the students will face when they enter employment in private industry. Any other type of situation does not do justice to the student or the occupation. But, it is essential that the setting be conducive to the teaching-learning situation. The main purpose of the shops or laboratories in our schools is that of providing instructional teaching-learning situations for students.

From time to time, the wise instructor might ask for student comments on what could be done to improve the shop. Remember, the shop is designed for learners and any inputs, as far as improvements are concerned, should be worthy of consideration.

The Lesson Plan

Lesson plan construction and format were discussed in detail in chapter seven. Figure 7–2 presented an example outline of a lesson plan. The lesson plan format is consistent with the individual instructional units recommended for the course of study and discussed in chapter six.

By this time, you should have had an opportunity to prepare a lesson plan or two using the suggested format or a modified version of it. The concern now is to present the lesson, making use of the lesson plan that you have prepared. If CCTV or VTR equipment is available, it would be a good idea to tape your presentation and then play it back for self-evaluation. If video equipment is not available, at the very least, it is suggested that you audio tape your lesson presentation. For purposes of this book, the lesson presentation to be described will be based upon the lesson plan format suggested in chapter seven.

The Presentation

The outline of the presentation will be based upon the following lesson plan format.

Title page
Introductory statement
Behavioral objectives
References
Instructional aids
The presentation (instructional content)
Discussion — questions
Application
Evaluation criteria

The material to follow will be presented in procedural order, which is not based on time sequence.

Introductory Statement.   It is the opening remarks that will set the stage for what is to follow. The introductory statement should be carefully worded when first written in the lesson plan; it should then be used as written during the presentation. The statement should be concerned with the necessity or importance of the lesson to be presented. Think of yourself as a salesman selling a product, which is the lesson. You might briefly review what preceded and what will follow the lesson.

Behavioral Objectives.   You, no doubt, spent considerable time in writing the behavioral objectives that appear now in your lesson plan. Let the students know what behavior (this refers to performance, not discipline) will be expected of them after the lesson presentation. In basic terms, you are indicating what technique will be used to evaluate their performance when you state the one or more behavioral objectives for the lesson. If the lesson topic is the use of the Weston Model 611 tube tester, one objective might be: "The student, given a Weston Model 611 tube tester, should be able to test and indicate the condition of a conventional vacuum tube within 2 minutes and do it successfully 90 percent of the time." (Underlined numbers may vary accordingly.) This should indicate to the students that if given a Weston Model 611 tube tester and one conventional vacuum tube, that within a two minute period, they should be able to check and indicate the condition of the tube and be correct 90 percent of the time (nine out of ten in twenty minutes). The students then would realize what level of performance on such an objective is expected of them. The teacher would have to provide sufficient equipment, tubes, and class time to allow the students to practice. A student would clearly know when he reached the level of performance expected and at that time, ask the teacher to evaluate his performance.

References.   It is a good idea to let the students know what references on the lesson are available both in the shop and elsewhere. Such references might include textbooks, instructional manuals, charts, single-concept films, trade publications, etc. It would be to your advantage to have a few example references that you used available to show and share with the students. If you like the idea of using the lesson plan as an information sheet, the students will then receive a copy of the plan for their notebooks.

Instructional Aids.   The instructional aids are indicated in the lesson plan and may or may not be an actual part of the lesson presentation. Much will depend upon the type or types of instructional aids or materials that you have decided to use. If a 16 mm film is to be used along with your lesson, you would indicate the title of the film, supplier, and running time. It would be obvious to the students in the class that the film was being used as an instructional aid. It is included on the lesson plan to remind the teacher that the film, projector, and screen are all essential to the lesson.

If the instructional aid used is an information sheet, a copy should be attached to the lesson plan. The information sheet could very well be the most important ingredient in the lesson. The teacher would want to make certain that sufficient copies are readily available for the students. Your lesson plan itself may very well be a form of information sheet if you want to use it as such.

The instructional aids that you have selected to use should be of help to you in making the presentation. They should be of value to the students in making the lesson content easier to understand and easier to apply to their actual performance activities.

The wise teacher will attempt to use a variety of aids and not rely on only one type. Too much of any one type might lose its effectiveness after a while. The selection of instructional aids is but one item in your instructional strategy.

The Presentation (Instructional Content).   Many different types of strategies have been suggested for this section of the lesson plan. They boil down to the presentation of the instructional content in a logical sequential order. The procedure you select can, and should, vary with your teaching style. Nothing is wrong with a simple numerical listing of topics or items which are essential to the demonstration. Systematic procedure proceeding from the most simple to the most complex ingredients should be presented in procedural order.

You might highlight or underline the most essential elements of your lesson plan by underlining various key words. You should be encouraged to experiment with a number of ways to construct this section of the lesson plan and then present the lesson. After all, lesson plans are for the use of teachers and to be most effective must suit the teaching style of the individual teacher.

A good lesson requires the teacher to have a thorough knowledge of the material he is about to present to the class. It includes a definite plan of procedure which should be the lesson plan.

A good presentation will include interwoven questions to check the understanding of the students as the presentation moves along. Safety instruction, if appropriate, should be included with the material that is being presented to the students. The short-range and long-range objectives of the lesson should be tied in with the presentation.

Discussion — Questions.   It is a good idea to summarize the presentation by one technique or another. One way is to prepare five or more questions which can be asked of the students at the conclusion of the lesson. Questions can be selected that will attempt to summarize the lesson as well, and give the teacher some feedback information concerning how well the students understood the lesson. The questions can cause additional questions to be raised and a discussion may logically develop.

Application.   Immediate reinforcement of the demonstration or lesson should be built into the lesson plan and the presentation. This can be referred to as the application phase. If the presentation was important enough to be made in the first place, then immediate application of the presentation should be required of the students.

If a lesson dealing with Ohm's law is the topic of the presentation, then the application might be to require the students to work out a number of Ohm's law problems. If the presentation was a demonstration lesson on the use of the cross-cut saw, then the application might be actual supervised practice requiring the students to use the cross-cut saw. Whatever application is involved, it should be consistent with the stated behavioral or performance objectives.

Due to the very nature of most shop and laboratory subjects, the "hands-on" type of application is a very important phase of the instructional teaching-learning situation. Usually, each succeeding lesson or demonstration builds on what preceded it. Shop and laboratory teachers have long made use of progress charts which indicate both to the student and teacher, what progress has been made. In many cases, such progress charts reflect behavioral or performance objectives and are nothing new to shop and laboratory teachers.

Application should occur as soon as possible after the presentation if the most advantage is to be gained from the presentation.

Evaluation Criteria.   When you list the various behavioral or performance objectives on your lesson plan, you more or less are indicating to the students what measure you expect them to reach. The evaluation criteria should be consistent with the stated behavioral or performance objectives. Any other form of evaluation is unfair, and students would soon lose faith in you.

Objective criteria should rule your decision regarding evaluation criteria. Subjective judgement has little room in shop and laboratory teaching. Action verbs should be your key in writing objectives and in selecting evaluation criteria. Words such as the following and many others will prove helpful: list, calculate, identify, locate, design, draw, calibrate, install, replace, repair, inspect, service.

Using the example based on a presentation of a lesson on Ohm's law, one method of evaluation might be as follows:

> The student should be able to mathematically calculate correctly, to the nearest tenth, nine out of ten *simple* Ohm's law problems. (Simple might refer to no value larger than 10 or less than .001.)

The teacher must be conscious of good speaking habits, good posture, and mannerisms at all times within the shop and laboratory. He must be constantly on the alert for ways to evaluate his teaching ability and improve his teaching style. The improvement of one's self should be given high priority by all teachers. How would you like to be a student in your own class?

Application and Follow-Up

Each presentation should be followed by hands-on or practical application of the lesson content. In most cases, the shop or laboratory instructor will probably give demonstration type lessons. Such lessons should require practice of a hands-on nature as soon as possible after the lesson. The teacher would move about the shop giving individual assistance, as needed, to the students.

Theory lessons should also require application in the form of added reading or written assignments consistent with the stated performance objectives. Follow-up by the teacher is essential. The teacher should review the presentation he made Monday before starting his presentation on Tuesday.

DISCUSSION QUESTIONS

1. Discuss, in small groups, the use of behavioral or performance objectives in shop and laboratory teaching. List the advantages and disadvantages of using such objectives.

2. Discuss, in small groups, the various techniques suggested for self-evaluation. List any other techniques that the group considers useful.

3. Discuss and make a model questionnaire with which students could evaluate teachers. Try it in your shop and report back to the group on its usefulness.

ASSIGNMENTS

1. Prepare a ten minute demonstration lesson plan. Present the lesson to this class next week.

2. Tape record one of your actual lessons during the week and bring the tape to class next week. It should not be less than ten minutes or longer than twenty minutes.

3. List your strongest and weakest abilities as you view them yourself. What might you do to improve the weaknesses?

ADDITIONAL REFERENCES

Estabrooke, Edward and R. Randolph Karch, *250 Teaching Techniques*. Milwaukee: The Bruce Publishing Co., 1956.

Leighbody, Gerald B. and Donald M. Kidd, *Methods of Teaching Shop and Technical Subjects*. Albany, New York: Delmar Publishers, Inc., 1966.

Proctor, James O. and G. Edward Griefzue, *TNT—Techniques, Notes, Tips for Teachers*. Albany, New York: Delmar Publishers, Inc., 1949.

Rose, Homer C., *The Instructor and His Job*. Chicago: American Technical Society, 1966.

U.S. Department of Health, Education and Welfare, *The Preparation of Occupational Instructors*. Washington, D.C.: U.S. Government Printing Office, 1966.

Chapter 11 INDIVIDUALIZATION OF INSTRUCTION

In chapter nine, considerable attention was placed on individual differences of students. If you agree that individuals vary in their ability, desire, and attitude toward learning, then it should make sense that no one technique will meet the individual needs of all the students in your shop or laboratory.

The teacher who is aware of the individual differences of the students in his class should attempt to individualize his instruction. The teacher should provide the necessary hardware and software to allow each student to progress at his own rate. Such a procedure might be referred to as *individual pacing* or *self-pacing*. Many shop and laboratory teachers individualize their teaching by the varied conditions that exist in their classrooms. It is seldom that an observer walks into a shop and finds all the students doing exactly the same thing. In most cases, the students are working on live work (automotive mechanics, cosmetology) or on project-centered work (machine shop, carpentry). Such activity type procedures are related to performance objectives established for the students.

Definition

Two examples come to mind as being illustrative of individualized instruction. One is that of the driver education instructor teaching the car phase of his course. His concern is the one student behind the wheel. This is a one-to-one relationship between student and teacher. Another example is the flight instructor working with the student pilot.

Such situations that are essential for driver education and flight training are not practical and much too costly for other areas of instruction. The teacher can attempt to individualize instruction within the group. The teacher of air conditioning with fifteen students in his class can attempt to work individually with each student. It is something that the teacher must want to do and work at to be successful. It takes a high level of instructional skill on the part of the teacher and the cooperation of the students to make the most of the procedure.

Individualized instruction is not a new concept. It is a technique that was suggested and used many years ago. The technique is especially useful to the shop or laboratory teacher due to the "hands on" nature of the teaching-learning situation. The improved instructional materials in the form of audiovisual devices make individualized instruction a more useful technique than it was in the past.

If you attempt to individualize instruction in your shop or laboratory, you are basically attempting to custom tailor the learning experiences of each student within the class. Some students will progress faster and further than others. But this is as it should be if you are aware of individual differences. It is your responsibility to encourage each student to progress as far as he is able.

Self-Pacing

The shop or laboratory teacher who has made use of the progress chart has in a way been using a form of individual or self-pacing instruction. Self-pacing is basically a technique that allows and encourages each student to advance at his own rate. It takes into consideration the factor of individual differences. Correspondence courses are probably one of the best examples of an individual or self-pacing concept that we can consider. The student can move as fast or slow as he desires to complete the course. Much, no doubt, depends on the student's motivation and time available to work on the lesson.

The teacher can attempt to provide a teaching-learning situation that encourages such a self-pacing concept. The concept is compatible with the course of study design and behavioral or performance objectives discussed in earlier chapters. The unit technique of course of study development places the subject content in procedural order starting with the most simple and proceeding to the most complex. The unit technique makes use of well written behavioral or performance objectives and opens the door to an individual or self-pacing concept within the shop or laboratory.

Such a system of self-pacing instruction would give the student a clear picture of his rate of progress within the shop. It would allow each student to progress at his own rate and even, perhaps, complete a three-year program in two years or less. If earlier completion were not possible, due to administrative red tape, the student could go into still more advanced level work within his specialization. Likewise, the slow student might take four years to complete the requirements that normally take three years. But this is not objectionable as long as his level of performance and skill are developed to make him employable.

A minimum amount of time would be spent in lectures and a maximum amount of time in individual instruction in a teaching-learning situation which encourages individual or self-pacing instruction. The teacher would be a resource person and manager of the instructional facility. His importance would be just as great, but his role somewhat different than the traditional type teacher.

Suggested Techniques

The following activities are some that you may find usable in your teaching assignment. They can be used in various ways to individualize instruction in shop and laboratory teaching.

Course of Study.   When behavioral or performance objectives are used on students evaluated in terms of the stated objectives, the individual approach to teaching has been used. Each student is evaluated in terms of the objectives he is able to master and not in terms of the performance of his fellow students.

The individual or self-pacing concept can also function if the teacher is willing to allow and encourage students to advance at their own rates. If a student completes Unit X, he should be allowed to immediately start the next unit and not have to wait until the rest of the class completes Unit X. A teacher may very well have students working on four or five different units at the same time, but this is to be expected due to individual differences and levels of motivation.

The Project.   An important and helpful way of individualizing instruction is by means of the project method. The project in a machine shop course might be to construct a C clamp to meet certain assigned specifications. The project is not the end product but is only a means to an end. The main purpose should be the performance objectives that a student must meet in order to end up with a properly machined and constructed C clamp. The selection of projects should be closely coordinated with the performance objectives.

Project work makes it necessary for the teacher to move from student to student and work with each student individually. At times, it will be necessary to call the entire class together for a lesson or demonstration. At other times, you may want to work with a small group of students on a particular problem that they are having that is of mutual interest to them all.

Live work.   Automotive mechanics, cosmetology, food service, television repair, and other specializations are able to use "live" work in the instructional program. Many automotive mechanics teachers will operate their shop just like a shop in an automobile agency. The teacher is like the service manager in an agency and must stand accountable for the work turned out.

Before taking on live work, be sure you check out any state or local regulations that might apply. Use special care in determining legal liability in the event of damage to property or injury to an individual. Most boards of education will have established policies regarding live work in the shops and laboratories.

Some schools operate walk-in tea shops which are used as teaching situations for food service students. Walk-in school barber shops, bakeries, and beauty parlors are not uncommon to vocational education programs.

Such activities do individualize instruction as well as create real and not simulated situations for students. Students repair, replace, locate trouble, or provide some form of service rather than end up with a finished product such as in the project method.

Some specializations can and should use a combination of live work and project work. It would be best for the beginning automotive mechanics student to first do some project type work on "dead" jobs (perhaps school owned vehicles, especially for this purpose) before doing any live work. The same would apply to the barbering, cosmetology, and television repair students.

Experimentation.   The experiment approach can be a suitable alternative to project or live work in some areas of instruction. Electronics is one subject in which a series of experiments designed to take a student from one level to another can be used with a high degree of success. Behavioral or performance objectives can and should be built into the experimental approach.

Teacher-made experiments would be more relevant to the local situation than. would be some purchased book of experiments. Each student or students in groups of two to four, would work on the experiments and progress from one experiment to the next at their own rate.

With more advanced students, the "experiment in reverse" might be worthy of your consideration. The student or group of students is charged with the responsibility of developing an experiment. In other words, they set out to prove a concept or law by means of writing an experiment, rather than just being handed an experiment to complete.

Programmed instruction.   As more and more programmed instruction books and materials are published, teachers should be aware as to what is available in their teaching area. Such materials can help in remedial as well as in supplemental instruction within the shop or laboratory.

Programmed materials appropriate to the objectives of the course can help to individualize the instructional process. They have the unique advantage of allowing students to progress at their own rate while periodically testing the students on past information. With the supportive hardware devices, the instructional system can even be a hands-on experience for the students, much like that found in correspondence courses in electronics and other areas. A teacher who has received some basic instruction in programmed learning techniques can write his own programmed materials to suit the goals of a particular course.

Independent study.   Individual independent study projects or assignments can be arranged between the teacher and student. The special interests of the student can result in some particular type of project or research effort on his part. Each student selects his own topic then carries out the project. He consults with the teacher when it is necessary.

The independent study topic is decided upon as a result of some pupil-teacher planning and should have some stated objective. In this sense, some form of contract should exist between both parties so that each knows what is expected of the other.

Role playing.   Role playing can be an excellent technique for understanding ourselves and others in the roles we play and for practicing interpersonal in-group skills. The technique places the student in the position of a person who is very different from the student.

The role playing technique can be of special value in shop and laboratory teaching in the area of employer-employee relations. The employment interview, on-the-job relations with other employees, and special other uses can be suitable to the technique.

The role playing is directed by the teacher, and the scene resulting might be in response to something that happened in the shop. Perhaps a violation of a shop safety rule occurred. The implications could be used in a role playing situation to see how the matter would have been resolved had it occurred in industry rather than the school.

Small group instruction.   As indicated earlier, it is not essential to always have a one to one ratio for individual instruction. Every time the instructor calls together a small group of students for a demonstration or discussion, individualization of instruction is taking place.

Project work, live work, and experiments can all be used within the small group process. The teacher must use care in the selection of the group members. The more advanced students might function as group leaders and be of real assistance to the slower members. As a teacher gets to know the students in his class, he will soon find out which students can best work together and which ones cannot.

Video-tape recorder (VTR).   If closed circuit television equipment (CCTV) and/or video tape recording equipment (VTR) are available, both can be useful to the teacher attempting to individualize instruction. Demonstration lessons can be video-taped by the instructor and made available for student viewings. If a student was absent on the day the lesson was given or just wanted to review the lesson, it could be played back for him at a convenient time. More and more schools are being equipped with CCTV and VTR equipment to assist in the instructional process.

Computer assisted instruction.   Considerable time and money are being spent on electronic computers which provide for various kinds of feedback and branching based on the student's immediate and earlier replies and other data. Different models use electronic typewriters and push buttons which make it possible to hold a question until the student gets it right. Computer assisted instruction is a very advanced form of programmed instruction making use of an electronic computer, but having many unique advantages. Properly prepared programs can help to individualize the instructional process especially in the related theory area of shop instruction.

Single concept films.   As the name implies, each film is concerned with one concept. They seem to be of particular value in demonstration type lessons where a student is required to develop a certain level of manual skill. The continuous film can be reviewed over and over again, until the student masters the subject matter.

The teacher who desires can make his own films if he takes the time. Some commercial single concept films can also be purchased.

Problem solving.   The problem solving technique can be used in the shop to encourage creativity as well as a way to individualize the instructional process. The teacher can have the students form groups, each group working on the same or a different problem. The problems might concern labor-management questions, design of some product, redesign of an existing product, current labor problems, etc.

This is an ideal situation because the teacher is working with each student in his class, recognizing individual differences and attempting to encourage each student to advance to his maximum.

DISCUSSION QUESTIONS

1. Discuss how you presently take into account the individual differences of the students in your shop or laboratory when grading (evaluating) their performance.

2. List the advantages and disadvantages of the self-pacing concept.

3. Divide the class into small groups by subject matter specialization. Each group should prepare a list of the techniques that could be used within their specialization to individualize instruction.

ASSIGNMENTS

1. Evaluate the performance of the students in your shop, laboratory, or class. List, by number (not name), each student in your class. What unique characteristic that might be considered an individual difference have you noticed in your students? What, if anything, have you done to adjust your teaching strategy to the situation?

2. List the things that you do or could do to individualize the instruction in your class.

3. What might you do to implement an individual or self-pacing system in your class? List the items.

ADDITIONAL REFERENCES

Alexander, William, *et al. Independent Study in Secondary Schools.* New York: Holt, Rinehart & Winston, Inc., 1967.

Draper, Dale C., *Educating for Work*. Washington, D.C.: National Association of Secondary School Principals, 1967.

Skinner, B. F., *The Technology of Teaching*. New York: Appleton-Century-Crofts, 1968.

U.S. Department of Health, Education, and Welfare. *New Directions in Vocational Education*. Washington, D.C.: U.S. Government Printing Office, 1967.

Chapter 12 INSTRUCTIONAL AIDS

Definition

Instructional aids are devices of one nature or another that can be used by the teacher in the instructional process. They make it possible for the teacher to make his lessons or demonstrations much more interesting to the students. It is much easier to demonstrate to a class how to use a cross-cut saw than it is to tell them how to use one. The cross-cut saw and lumber to be cut are therefore instructional aids. Training aids have been used for many years and perhaps date to the time the first caveman drew pictures on the wall of his cave.

Instructional aids include such things as information sheets, working models, overhead projectors, electronic teaching devices, and simulators such as used in driver training or flight instruction. Chalkboards, flannel boards, closed circuit television, and films are also considered instructional aids.

This chapter will attempt to cover a wide range of instructional aids that may be of value to shop and laboratory teachers. Operational details of the equipment will not be discussed since such information can be found in instructional manuals and books dealing with the particular aid in question. The reason for including this chapter on instructional aids is to help the beginning or experienced teacher get an overview of the types of instructional aids that are available and how they can be used in the instructional process. Many of the aids will prove extremely valuable to the teacher who is attempting to individualize the instructional process in his shop or laboratory.

Why Use Instructional Aids?

An instructional aid is a device to help in the instructional process: the teaching-learning situation. A good teacher will not use the aid with the intention of replacing his good teaching methods but to supplement his teaching skill and aid the student to grasp and utilize the material. Instructional aids should only be used if they are appropriate and suitable to the needs of the teacher and learner and serve to improve the teaching-learning situation.

Much research has been conducted dealing with various types of instructional materials and media (training aids). Most have found better and more effective results in the teaching of many subjects. Almost any subject can be enhanced through the use of teaching media such as the instructional aids available to us today. The wide range of both hardware and software devices on the market today indicate wide acceptance by those in the marketing field. However, the individual teacher must use care in selecting what will best meet his instructional needs.

An instructional aid will not necessarily make teaching any easier. However, the instructional aid may help the teacher to teach a particular lesson much more effectively or solve a particular problem with ease. Instructional aids, if properly selected by the teacher, have the following characteristics.

1. They should prove valuable for all ability and age groups.
2. They can bring experts and many multiple resources to the classroom and/or shop.
3. They should be able to obtain and hold the attention of almost all learners.
4. They should induce greater acquisition and longer retention of factual information.
5. They should be able to show otherwise unavailable processes, materials, events, and things.
6. They can illustrate and help clarify non-verbal symbols and images.
7. They can illustrate and help clarify specific details.
8. They can bring modern industrial practices into the shop or classroom.

Selection of Instructional Aids

The selection of instructional aids depends on a number of things.

Subject matter
Student interests and tastes
Lesson or course objectives
Physical location—lighting, seating, etc.
Class size
Budget

You should be able to find a number of instructional aids to meet your needs and stay within your budget. The availability of the hardware associated with instructional aids is a major factor to be considered by the teacher. It makes little sense to order transparencies for an overhead projector unless an overhead projector is available to the teacher for classroom use.

In selecting instructional aids, the teacher might ask himself the following questions.

1. Does the aid deal with the important curricular content?
2. Is the aid the best one on the market on a dollar-for-dollar basis?
3. Is the aid suited for students of the age level with whom you are planning to use it?
4. Is the item up-to-date and accurate?
5. Is the aid suitable for individual, small-group, or large-group instruction?
6. Is it worth the money it costs and the time required to use it?
7. Has the manufacturer run any studies to determine the relative advantages of the instructional aid? What is the research evidence found?
8. Is the aid technically satisfactory?
9. If it is possible, try out the item before purchasing it. Has student reaction been obtained and recorded?
10. Is the item the best available and the best way to present the subject matter to the students?

On the basis of the previous questions and their answers, you should be able to select the most suitable instructional aid for your purposes. Do not be afraid to request your administrator to purchase both equipment and supplies of an instructional nature. But be prepared to justify their need if you are requested to do so. If your first request is not approved, continue to re-submit it if you can justify its use. The surest way not to get what you want is to not re-submit a requisition that was not approved the first time.

Many vocational schools are sadly lacking in the area of instructional aids of an audiovisual nature, while others are well equipped. The teachers must make known their needs, and when the equipment is available, make sure it is well used in the instructional process.

Classification of Instructional Aids

Instructional aids generally can be classified into four groups.

Visual Instructional Aids.   This group consists of demonstration boards, chalkboards, flip charts, bulletin boards, models, silent films, single-concept films, slides, projected material of a silent nature, and filmstrips. They all have one thing in common in that no sound is provided with them.

Auditory Instructional Aids.   AM and FM radio, all types of tape recordings, or records can be classified as audio instructional aids. They all have one thing in common in that only sound is provided to the learner.

Audiovisual Instructional Aids.   This area includes sound motion pictures, television, combination record with filmstrip, or tape with slide series or filmstrip. Such aids include sound with a visual display of one sort or another.

Simulation Instructional Aids.   Classroom driver trainers and aircraft simulators are two primary examples of simulation type instructional aids. This category includes all instructional devices used to simulate the real life situation.

Various Instructional Aids

This review of a number of instructional aids is intended only to give a brief overview. Additional information and operational details can be found in books and manufacturers' materials that would describe the aids in greater detail. No attempt has been made to place them in any sequence.

The Chalkboard.   The chalkboard is, for many teachers, the most frequently used instructional aid. The chalkboard is only as good an instructional aid as the person who uses it. The instructor only needs some simple drawing skills and some imagination to make effective use of the board. Chalkboards now come in a variety of colors including white. With the white it is possible to use a felt tipped marking pen to write on the board. A white board can also be used as a screen for projected materials.

The instructor's technique in the use of the chalkboard is very important. It is very easy to find yourself talking to the chalkboard rather than the class. Simply watch yourself and the technique that you use in the use of the chalkboard.

Demonstration Boards. Demonstration boards come in a variety of types including flannel and magnetic types. They can be effectively used to progressively build elements of a presentation (schematic diagram, systems technique, etc.). All require the speaker to physically handle the subject material, adding interest to a relative static presentation. It is necessary to prepare in advance the material to be used with the various demonstration boards. The boards can be used very effectively for lessons which are video taped.

Poster-type Displays. These include charts, diagrams, maps, illustrations, bulletin board displays, and other materials large enough for the class to see. Most schools already have some of these. Manufacturers and sales organizations also have many available, often free to schools. Investigate poster possibilities through your school and trade connections. These types of materials can be quite beneficial in complementing the presentation of the instructor.

Flip Charts. Flip charts include flipovers, easel cards, dropdowns, and portfolios. Bound presentations are used when a rigid, prescribed sequence is desired. The more flexible loose card forms are desirable when a tailor-made, personalized approach necessitates adding, deleting, or changing the order of the cards. The size of the flip chart limits the size of the group with which it may be effectively used. The charts and presentation must be set up in advance. Types of presentations are limited only by the imagination.

Information or Instructional Sheets. This group includes any instructional aid containing factual information as to nomenclature, materials, tools, equipment, processes, and theory indicating why things are done. This category can include such things as assignment sheets, operation sheets, and job sheets.

The sheets are usually teacher made, run off on a ditto, mimeograph, or some other type of duplicating process, and given to the students. Additional information can be given as needed and the sheets placed in the students' notebooks.

Assignment sheets are used to give the learner definite work to do for the application or practice step of a lesson. They should be very specific, adding detailed explanation when necessary.

An operation sheet usually gives detailed step-by-step instructions for performing a single operation or the acquiring of a single skill.

A job sheet usually lists the major operations, in order of performance, that are required to do a complete job which involves a number of separate operations. Such sheets should supplement the instructional procedure and not duplicate material readily available in textbooks.

Study Guide. This is an instructional aid used to provide a means for individual instruction in classroom teaching, either to allow for individual progress in a class where the students are at the same level or when the class is made up of students at various levels or in different occupations.

Textbooks–Reference Library. Books, magazines, pamphlets, and manufacturer's catalogs are all instructional aids. For the instructor's own use, every kind and form of printed material that may be useful for his teaching should be investigated. The teacher should use a high degree of selectivity in picking out the textbooks for the class. He should pick out the one that best suits the needs and stated objectives of his course. All too often, the greatest influence on curriculum has been the textbooks available. Your course of study is the key, not the textbook. Pick out the book which most completely covers the material in your course of study. Do not let the book be your only guide and set the direction that the course will follow.

Motion Picture Films. One of the most effective instructional aids is the motion picture film. The motion picture is the nearest thing to personal experience and is the most professional of the completely packaged presentations. No other audiovisual aid combines the versatility, clarity, and dramatic impact of motion pictures. The fluidity of motion pictures enhances many stories. Use it when a more dramatic program is in order, when no sequence changes are needed, and when you can afford it.

From an instructional standpoint, the motion picture offers many advantages not found in other audiovisual aids. Motion picture photography makes it possible to speed up slow processes or slow down fast action.

Many films are available on a cost free basis and others on a rental basis. Your school should have catalogs which list what films are available to suit your needs.

Always preview any film you plan to use before showing it to a class. This procedure, although it takes your time, might save valuable instructional time. The film might not be suited to the needs of your class, and of limited value. The film might have breaks in it that require repair. Always make sure that the film and projector are both in good operating condition.

Filmstrips. A filmstrip is a series of still images that are photographed in sequence on a roll of film. Some filmstrips are available with synchronized sound on record or tape. Projectors are available which include a record player. Other filmstrips are available with a booklet which can be used by the instructor to explain the various slides.

The projector itself consists of a reflective mechanism which conveys the film to the student by use of a screen. It is lightweight and relatively inexpensive. It is easily carried from room to room. Prepared filmstrips can be purchased relating to various subject areas.

Slide Projector. The slide projector is similar in its function to the previously discussed filmstrip projector. It offers lightweight characteristics, adaptability, ease of operation, and flexibility in regard to material shown. This characteristic of flexibility makes it superior to the filmstrip picture as sequence of material can be arranged, deleted, or changed.

Instructor prepared materials are also a possibility with the slide projector. The machine uses slides made from 35 mm film which is very commonly used by amateur photographers.

In recent years, great improvements have been made in slide projectors. With the proper equipment, sound on tape can be automatically synchronized to the slide. It is best to review the catalogs of the various projector companies before making a purchase.

Opaque Projector. This type of projector shows on a screen the image from a book page or similar source. Thus, material not on slides or films can be projected on a screen in the room.

An open form of opaque projector permits the instructor to write or draw on a transparent sheet in the machine. Thus, the enlarged picture grows on the screen as the lesson proceeds. Copy for opaque projection can be prepared by the instructor.

A third variation of the opaque projector will project an enlarged silhouette of a solid object on the screen. This can be an aid in inspection and instruction especially for details or small tolerances not readily seen without enlargement.

Overhead Projector. The overhead projector transmits a strong beam of light through a transparent material and onto a screen behind the instructor at the front of the room. The instructor, facing the class, and to the side of the projector, can point, write or draw on the transparency, and the material is projected on the screen as he does so.

Overhead projectors are designed for speaker operation. By adding overlays or removing opaque flaps, the speaker can exploit the dramatic qualities of progressive disclosure.

Transparencies can be purchased from a good number of companies in a wide number of subject areas. Transparencies can be prepared in black and white, single colors or any number of colors. This can be done photographically, manually (grease pencil), or on some type of office copying machines.

Each and every classroom or shop should have an overhead projector in it. It is of course, essential that the school provide the necessary supplies (software) to assist the teacher in making his own transparencies.

Single Concept Films.   Single concept films are usually three or four minutes in length. Each film is contained in its own plastic cartridge which slides conveniently into the single concept projector. This eliminates problems related to threading or rewinding, since the film is continuous and the cartridge can be placed or removed from the projector at any time.

Single concept films focus their attention on individual segments of subject matter. They are especially of value for individual or small group instruction.

A number of companies are producing single concept films which are suitable for various vocational programs. It is also possible to produce your own 8 mm film and have it packaged in the plastic cartridge.

Single concept films can free the teacher from the tedious task of repeating demonstrations and permit him to add a creative dimension to his teaching. They should be of special value to the teacher who is attempting to individualize the instructional process.

Mock-ups.   These are simplified arrangements of the real parts, usually mounted on boards or stands so that the essential parts work together normally. The teaching advantage is that non-essential parts do not distract from the specific topics being studied. Mock-ups may sometimes be brought into a classroom when it would not be possible to show the actual parts of assemblies.

Models.   Models are imitations of real objects. They may be enlargements of the real object or made to smaller scale. Scale models can be used effectively to show relation of one part to another. Working models can show relation of action and movement of parts. Caricature models can be used to identify and give extra emphasis to important details. Such models can attract special attention by exaggeration.

Three-dimensional aids may also be available through school and trade contacts. In many cases, it is often necessary to make them.

Closed Circuit Television (CCTV). The simplest television circuit connects a camera with a single receiver. Closed circuit television by cable may reach a number of locations in nearby rooms and buildings or even at greater distances. In recent years many schools have built in the necessary wiring for closed circuit television capabilities. CCTV programs can be devoted not only to direct instruction of students, but also to system-wide teachers meetings, to preview new instructional materials and in-service teacher education programs.

If your school is equipped with CCTV equipment, it will pay you to find out what services and facilities are available for your use. Additional study on your part would be essential in order for you to understand the many uses of CCTV. This self-study on your part should benefit your instructional process and improve the teaching-learning situation.

Video-Tape Recorders (VTR). Video-tape recording equipment in its simplest form consists of a camera, receiver, and video-tape recorder. It allows you to video-tape and play back as needed. Portable, light weight video-tape recorders are now available for a cost well within the budget of most schools. The equipment is easy to operate and can be moved from room to room as needed.

The VTR has many uses and should be of value to the shop and laboratory teacher. Industrial visitations or processes can be video-taped in industry and then viewed in the school shop or laboratory. A teacher can video-tape a lesson and then replay it as many times as needed by the students. The taped rerun can also be of value to the teacher in evaluating his own teaching style. Self-evaluation is essential for all engaged in the teaching-learning situation.

Computer Assisted Instruction (CAI). If your school has the facilities for computer assisted instruction (CAI), try to work up an instructional program for your students. The computer is not intended to replace the teacher but only to assist him. The computer can respond only in the ways for which it has been programmed. The computer can supplement the instruction given by the teacher and relieve him of many routine teaching tasks. Additional self-study on your part would be essential if you have CAI equipment available in your school.

Auditory Training Aids. Radio, phonograph records, and audio tape are considered audio training aids. Without any picture, slide, or video presentation, they are limited as far as instructional uses in shop and laboratory teaching are concerned. If you find usable audio devices for your subject specialization, use them if suitable to your teaching-learning situation.

DISCUSSION QUESTIONS

1. Divide the class into a number of small groups. Ask each group to develop some sort of card system which can be maintained and used by the teacher to evaluate various instructional aids. The card design should be such as to allow for evaluation of the aid as well as a review of the major instructional content.

2. Divide the class into a number of small groups by specialization Ask each group to develop a list of the instructional aids that they have readily available to them in their various schools.

ASSIGNMENTS

1. Conduct an inventory of the instructional aids available in your school. For purposes of this question, only concern yourself with hardware such as movie projectors, VTR, tape recorders, etc. The inventory should include the number of each and its manufacturer.

2. Conduct an inventory of the instructional aids, both hardware and software, available in your shop or laboratory. This inventory should include charts, models, films, records, etc.

3. Design, build, or make one new instructional aid for your shop or laboratory. Bring it to class to show to the others and explain how you will plan to use it.

ADDITIONAL REFERENCES

Audiovisual Equipment Directory. Fairfax, Virginia: National Audiovisual Association, Inc., 1969.

Educational Films. East Lansing, Michigan: Michigan State University, 1969.

Educational Motion Pictures. Bloomington, Indiana: Audiovisual Center, Indiana University, 1970.

McGraw-Hill Films, 8mm. Film Loops, Records, Transparencies. New York: McGraw-Hill Films, 1970.

Multi-Media Instructional Material. New York: Universal Education and Visual Arts, 221 Park Avenue South, 1969.

Saterstrom, Mary H., ed., *Educators Guide to Free Science Materials.* Randolph, Wisconsin: Educators Progress Service, Inc., Revised annually.

Wittich, Walter A., ed., *Educators Guide to Free Tapes, Scripts, and Transscriptions.* Randolph, Wisconsin: Educators Progress Service, Inc., Revised annually.

Part IV EVALUATION

Chapter 13 CLASS RECORDS

Definition

Class records vary from school system to school system. There are no standard record forms which meet the needs of all schools. It is essential that you be made aware of the required class records for your school. Most shop instructors will find that two general classes of records are needed for the well organized and managed shop, those records required by national, state, or local regulations; and those needed by the teacher in the efficient management of his shop, laboratory, or classroom. Class records, therefore, are those required or "nice-to-have" records which make for the successful operation of the teaching-learning situation. The class records discussed in this chapter deal in the main with student progress and evaluation. Not of concern in this chapter are such things as staff-personnel records, financial records and materials, and equipment records or shop safety records.

You will have little control over those school required records. It will be to your advantage to get to understand the forms used and regiment yourself to the record keeping that is required by the system. This does not mean that after you are accustomed to the required record keeping system that you must be content with it. Most school administrators are willing to consider suitable alternatives if the alternative is better than the existing system. The record keeping time should be kept to a minimum and the instructional time to a maximum.

The Importance of Record Keeping

Record keeping that concerns itself with student performance and evaluation should be taken as very serious business. After hundreds of students pass through your shop and graduate, it becomes difficult to keep a mental picture of each one. You will be called upon by prospective and present employers of your past students to varify attendance, shop attitude, and shop skills that they exhibited while studying with you.

Good record keeping is essential in order to give a fair and honest appraisal of a student's performance in your shop. Such records and evaluation criteria should be consistent with the stated objectives of your school, department, and course. The evaluation criteria and associated records should be well understood by the students in the class.

If you are attempting to individualize the instructional process and make use of performance objectives, it is especially important that your record keeping system is consistent with your instructional strategy. The importance of accurate record keeping should be obvious. If performance objectives are used, the student should know when he moves from one objective to the next, and the class records should accurately reflect the movement. In many cases, you will have to design your own shop record keeping system to suit your needs and those of your students.

The Teacher's Responsibility

The major responsibility for record keeping within the school is placed with the principal. He, then, will delegate the various record keeping responsibilities to the administrative and teaching staff of the school. The teachers should be well informed at a yearly orientation session as to what records are required, how they should be maintained, and any due dates essential to an orderly process. Operational procedures for record keeping should be spelled out and clearly understood by the staff.

Since wide variations exist in required records from one school to another, it would make little sense to review record keeping in detail in this book. It is the teacher's responsibility to find out early in the school year all he can about the record keeping responsibilities that are his.

Whatever other records, other than those required, the teacher of shop or laboratory subjects finds necessary for the operation of the shop are his personal responsibility. But use care, it is easy to design a record or record system, but it is time consuming to record data on the records. Maintain only those records that are essential to the smooth operation of your teaching-learning situation.

Student Involvement in Record Keeping

Many administrators insist that all records which are of a personal nature be kept by the teacher or office clerks. This would include personal records, report cards, and health records, etc. In other schools, the policy might apply to only those records which are central office records. Still other administrators might require that all records including central office and classroom records be maintained by the teacher without any assistance from his students.

Before you involve students in the classroom, laboratory, or shop record keeping procedure, check out the school policy on record keeping. If students can have some involvement in the record keeping procedure, you might design some procedures to be used in your shop. This does not imply that any one student becomes a record clerk and thereby neglects his other assigned tasks.

Many jobs require some form of record keeping on the part of the employee. Certainly, students in particular specializations should be well acquainted with the typical paper work faced on-the-job. The record keeping responsibilities should be made as much a part of the total operation as possible.

At the minimum, consider assigning a record keeping clerk as one of the jobs of your shop personnel system. As such, he would be available ten or fifteen minutes each class session to assist in the record keeping procedures.

You, as the teacher, must stand accountable for the record keeping system. The work assigned to students in the record keeping system must be thoroughly planned, well explained, and adequately supervised by the teacher. The teacher must constantly stress the importance of neat and accurate record keeping.

School Required Records

The major concern of this chapter will focus on those necessary school records which involve student progress and evaluation. In most cases, you will have little control over the established procedures that are already in operation on a school wide basis.

ATTENDANCE RECORDS

Most schools will have a well established system for recording and reporting the attendance of students. The reporting procedure will vary from state to state depending upon the requirements and reporting procedures used. Many shop teachers will also be asked to serve from time to time as homeroom teachers. In the role of homeroom teacher, it usually is the teacher's responsibility to maintain an accurate record of the students assigned to his room. The procedures are usually well established, and it is the teacher's responsibility to learn the method that is being used within the system.

The shop or laboratory teacher or any teacher, as a matter of fact, should also want to maintain a record of attendance for students in his classes. Such records are of value to the teacher who might be asked to comment on the students' attendance and punctuality at a later time by an employer. Adequate records maintained by the teacher would yield the essential information. Usually the school will provide each teacher with a combination plan-attendance-grade book or other suitable materials for this type of record keeping.

STUDENT EVALUATION

This item is labeled as student evaluation due to the lack of a more suitable term. It is intended to refer to the day-to-day records that a teacher should maintain in order to accurately and fairly evaluate the performance of each student. In a sense, it relates to the grading system and reporting system used by the school system which is the next topic.

To complicate the issue still more, if you are structuring your course to meet individual students' needs and be "self-pacing" in nature, more problems might exist. If performance or behavioral objectives are being used, this will be a factor to be considered in the evaluation procedure. Your problem is to develop a record keeping system that is compatible with a system of individualized instruction and performance objectives and still usable within the school's reporting system.

It is difficult and perhaps impossible to use or illustrate one model that would be usable in more than one system. Whatever system is used, it should be very clearly explained to the students early in the school year and clearly understood by them. If the students do not understand the procedure, the system is worthless. It must relate and be compatible with the school's reporting system.

SCHOOL WIDE GRADING SYSTEM

Whatever evaluation system you use within your class, it must be compatible with the school wide grading system. You must be able to convert grades from your class to the school wide grading system. You may want to keep your grades in numerical values and then convert them to letter grades to be compatible with the school's grading system. The marking periods and final averaging methods also vary widely from school to school.

School A. This school uses a numerical grading system with 65 as the minimum passing average. Four ten-week marking periods are used to determine the final average.

10 week	20 week	30 week	40 week	final average

In such a grading system, it is possible for a student to pass during one marking period, fail the other three, and still pass the course on the basis of the final average. With ten-week grades of 80, 62, 62, and 62 the final average would be 66.5 which is passing. Likewise, a student could have a passing grade for three marking periods and a failing grade for one and fail the course on the final average. With ten-week grades of 66, 68, 70, and 50 the final average would be 63.5 which is failing.

In this system, the student who receives a very low grade during the first ten-week marking period, stands little change of passing the course. It might cause certain students to stop trying at all. Likewise, a student who receives a very high grade during the first marking period may be able to coast through the rest of the school year with a minimum amount of effort.

School B. This school uses a numerical grading system with 65 as the minimum passing average. Four ten-week marking periods plus the final examination are used to determine the final average.

10 week	20 week	30 week	40 week	final exam	final average

As you will note, each marking period plus the final examination has a value of 20 percent or one-fifth in determining the final average. If the final examination can be a performance type examination, the added advantage is a complete review of all the work covered during the school year. The system is subject to the same limitations as were discussed in the School *A* grading system.

School C.   This school uses a numerical grading system with 65 as the minimum passing average. Four ten-week marking periods are used in reporting student progress to the parents. A final examination is given, and the student must pass it to pass the course. In other words, no matter what the grades were for the four marking periods, the student must pass the final examination to pass the course. Such a system has some advantages and disadvantages just like any evaluation system. (a) The final examination must be proved valid and reliable. (b) A student who has done well all year, may have a bad day and fail the examination and the course. (c) The system would be some measure of final quality control, especially if performance objectives were used in the final examination. (d) A student could fail each quarter, yet pass the final examination and the course.

School D.   The system is the same as School *C,* except that a student who has a failing average for the four marking periods can pass the course if he passes the final examination. Such a system places success within reach of every student including those who may have done poorly most of the year.

School E.   The system is the same as School *B*, but uses a letter grade system.

OUTSTANDING	A	100–91
ABOVE AVERAGE	B	90–81
AVERAGE	C	80–71
BELOW AVERAGE	D	70–65
FAILING	E	64–

In reporting grades by means of a letter grade system, the teacher must use care in maintaining the numerical grades from which the letter grade was converted. A "C" may be a 71 or an 80, and the nine-point spread may be significant in determining the final average.

Review as completely as possible the school wide grading system in your school system. Make sure that you and your students have a full understanding of the system and how they will be evaluated.

CLASS RECORDS

Class records include both the school required records each teacher is expected to maintain and any additional records that the teacher wants to use.

Each teacher will find it necessary to record the progress of each student in his class book. It is in this book that the teacher records grades or the progress of each student, and this information will be used in reporting the progress of the student on the report card. The class book may also be used to record student attendance and tardiness.

The teacher must stand accountable for maintaining accurate class records. If asked to justify why a student got a certain grade, the teacher would be expected to produce suitable evidence to support the grade given. As indicated earlier, if grades are important, then the students must be kept fully informed as to their progress in the course. Students must be told very early in the school year how they will be evaluated in the course. The evaluation system must be fully explained by the teacher and understood by the students.

In addition to the school required class records, shop instructors may want to maintain one or more other additional types of records. One such record is a simple type of progress chart. One example of a simple progress chart is shown in Figure 13–1. The chart can be used for projects, experiments, performance objectives, or any additional use the teacher wants to use it for. In most vocational education shops, you will find some type of progress chart in use.

If you are using performance objectives in your course, you would simply indicate the objectives in the upper columns and the names of students in the proper column. The objectives could be indicated by number and the full statement of the objective in another chart or in a nearby notebook.

The progress chart, if properly used and maintained, can be very useful to the students and to the teacher. It very simply reports the progress being made by each student in the class. You should find it useful no matter what instructional strategy you use in the teaching-learning situation.

In addition to the progress chart, you might find some form of student appraisal sheet to be useful in your shop. Figure 13–2 is one example of a student appraisal sheet. It, to a large extent, indicates a subjective judgement of the student by the teacher. Your evaluation system will have to reflect if such subjective evaluation will be reflected in the grading system. It is included here not as an example that should be involved in evaluation, but only as a form that may be useful to the teacher. It is the writer's belief that evaluation must be based on clearly stated objectives. Subjective evaluations might be nice to have, but many variables can be involved that limit the value of such evaluations.

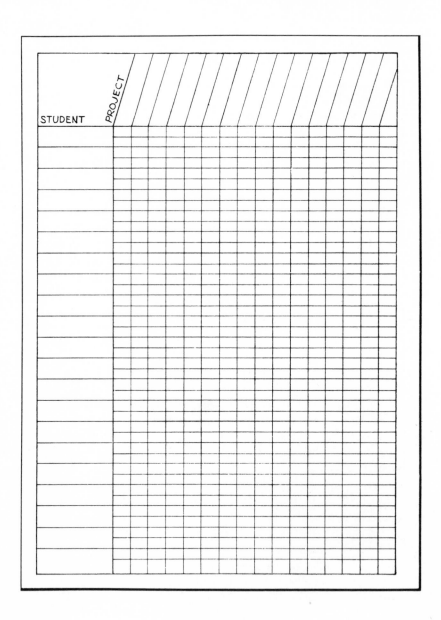

FIGURE 13–1

Progress Chart

STUDENT APPRAISAL SHEET

Name_____ Class_____ Date_____

Rated by_____ Score_____

ACCURACY OF SHOP AND CLASS WORK		ABILITY TO ACT AS A LEADER	
1. Makes many errors		1. Very dictatorial	
2. Is careless		2. Hinders	
3. Is fairly accurate		3. Fair	
4. Is careful		4. Good	
5. Is very accurate		5. Excellent	
CARE OF WORKING SPACE		ATTENDANCE	
1. Very untidy		1. Off a great deal no valid reason	
2. Careless		2. Off occasionally no valid reason	
3. Just passable		3. Off occasionally with valid reason	
4. Keeps space clean		4. Seldom off	
5. Space very clean and orderly		5. Never late or tardy	
HANDLING OF TOOLS AND EQUIPMENT		EXTRA ACTIVITIES	
1. Rough		1. Doesn't take part	
2. Careless		2. Seldom takes part	
3. Indifferent		3. Fair degree of participation	
4. Careful		4. Good degree of participation	
5. Very careful		5. Cooperates willingly, cheerfully	
SPEED IN SHOP AND CLASS		ATTITUDE TOWARDS CLASSMATES	
1. Very slow		1. Does not get along	
2. Slow		2. Looks down on them	
3. Ordinary		3. Neutral	
4. Fast		4. Good	
5. Very fast		5. Well liked, very cooperative	
USE OF WORKING TIME		ATTITUDE TOWARD TEACHERS	
1. Very wasteful		1. Disrespectful	
2. Loafs with others		2. Does not cooperate	
3. Passable		3. Average	
4. Busy		4. Cooperates	
5. Very busy		5. Very respectful, helpful	
USE OF MATERIALS		OBSERVANCE OF SAFETY RULES	
1. Wasteful		1. Disregards rules openly	
2. Careless		2. Disregards when not watched	
3. Fair		3. Average	
4. Good		4. Observes rules	
5. Very careful		5. Observes rules, has own rules too	
RESPONSIBILITY		ACCIDENT RECORD	
1. Buck passer		1. Many accidents thru carelessness	
2. Evades responsibility		2. Minor injuries thru carelessness	
3. Passable		3. Few minor injuries	
4. Likes it		4. Seldom injured	
5. Seeks it and handles it well		5. Never gets injured	
INITIATIVE		PERSONAL APPEARANCE, CLEANLINESS	
1. Doesn't exhibit any		1. Slovenly and dirty	
2. Very little		2. Untidy	
3. Average		3. Fair	
4. Offers many suggestions		4. Neat and clean	
5. Very original		5. Exceptionally pleasing	

Check only one item under each trait   Guidance and Placement Department
Middlesex County Vocational Schools

FIGURE 13–2

Student Appraisal Sheet

The Progress Chart

The progress chart was discussed in a limited fashion earlier in this chapter. Figure 13–1 is one example of a type of progress chart which is commonly used to plot the progress of each student within the class.

One must always be aware of the effect, if any, such a chart has on the slower students in the class. How would you like to have a record of your progress in a certain class on public display? A way around this might be to indicate a student assigned number on the chart rather than a name. Such a system allows each student to be aware of his progress in relation to the class, but shields the identity of the individual.

Individual progress charts for each student could be maintained as a class record by the teacher. Such an individual progress chart could be made available to the students on an individual basis. The student could, and should, in fact, maintain a copy of such a progress chart for his own information.

If you attempt to use behavioral or performance objectives in your course of study and your daily teaching, such a progress chart would be very valuable. The normal progression would be from the most simple to the most complex, and each student should be encouraged to progress at his or her own rate. The individual or group progress chart would give a clear indication of the progress of each student in the class.

If your course of study was constructed in the fashion suggested in chapter five and using performance objectives, the progress chart would give both the students and the teacher a clear indication of progress towards the final criterion measure of performance. Progress plotted and based on performance objectives would also prove of value to the future employer of the student. It would be a clear indication of the types of performance that the student had successfully demonstrated during his schooling. Such a record would mean much more to a prospective employer than a grade of A, B, or C. The progress chart used with a course of study based on performance objectives would tell what hands-on experiences the student had demonstrated, in a specified period of time and with what degree of success.

Student Numbers

You might want to consider assigning each student a student number to be used in your class. This technique has been highly successful with some teachers.

Such a student number system is useful for a number of purposes. It can be used in connection with the student personnel system or on the progress chart. Rather than posting the names of the various students in the class, a series of numbers known only to each student is recorded on the chart. It can also be used in explaining how term grades were arrived at. Each student knows where he stands in relation to his fellow students.

DISCUSSION QUESTIONS

1. Divide the class into a number of small groups. Each group should develop a model student evaluation system usable in a program using behavioral or performance objectives. Each of the small group chairmen should report back to the class on the model they developed.

2. Each class member should bring in a report card from the school district in which he is employed. If pre-service individuals are in the class, they should obtain cards from the school district in which they live. Discuss as a group the most common elements and the most dissimilar elements of the various cards.

3. Devise what the class considers the most suitable type of reporting form for shop and laboratory type programs. This should be a group effort under the leadership of one or more students.

ASSIGNMENTS

1. Make a progress chart that would be useful to you in your teaching assignment and with the course of study that you are currently using.

2. Bring in copies of the various records and/or forms that you are required to keep in your school. What other not-required-forms and/or records do you use?

3. Evaluate the *reporting system* and *report card* that is being used in your school system. Is it fair to students, parents, teachers, and employers? What modifications might make it more useful?

ADDITIONAL REFERENCES

Leighbody, Gerald B. and Donald M. Kidd, *Methods of Teaching Shop and Technical Subjects*. Albany, New York: Delmar Publishers, Inc., 1966.

Mager, Robert F. and Kenneth M. Beach, *Developing Vocational Instruction*. Palo Alto, California: Fearon Publishers, Inc., 1967.

Rose, Homer C., *The Instructor and His Job*. Chicago: American Technical Society, 1966.

Silvius, G. Harold and Estele H. Curry, *Teaching Successfully in Industrial Education*. Bloomington, Illinois: McKnight & McKnight Pub. Co., 1967.

Chapter 14 TESTING AND TEST CONSTRUCTION

The testing and test construction phases of your teaching assignment are very important. Testing is important as one technique of student evaluation as well as the improvement of the instructional process.

The Purpose of Tests

The teaching as well as the learning is measured by the testing procedure used by the teacher. Poor test scores by many students might indicate the need for the improvement of the instructional process on the part of the teacher.

There are two main reasons why we test or attempt to evaluate students: first, as a means to evaluate student ability and performance in order to provide the learner with a more accurate assessment of himself and his abilities, and second, as a means to indicate to the teacher how he might improve his instructional technique and materials.

The testing procedure itself then leads to evaluation of student performance and some method of reporting this evaluation to the student and his parents. Testing is the first phase; evaluation, the second phase.

Fair and accurate evaluation is not possible without some fair and suitable testing procedure. Both testing and evaluation should be based on some clearly stated objectives, otherwise the value of both are in doubt.

If tests are necessary, students have a right to know why. You, as the teacher, must be able to answer the following questions:

1. Why do I give tests?
2. Of what value are tests?
3. What type of test is best for my purposes?
4. Of what value are tests to my students?
5. When should I test?
6. How should I test?

Evaluation Based on Stated Objectives

All meaningful evaluation must be based upon some clearly defined objectives. It makes little sense to construct, administer, grade, and return a test to the students unless there was some purpose for it in the first place.

If you move from one state to another, you may be required to take another driver's test in order to obtain the proper driver's license. The objective of the test should be clear. You must pass the test before you will be granted the license. The test itself, at this point, is not important. The objective is the important thing. You must pass the test, be it written or performance (behind the wheel), in order to obtain the license.

In our schools, we should attempt to make educational objectives just as clear as in the previous example, realizing of course that no two students are exactly alike. Perhaps not all students will meet *all* the stated objectives, but most will satisfy the essential objectives. Those of us in occupational education should, and can, lead the way in this type of situation.

Clearly stated objectives concerning the test should be given to the students. They must know why they are required to take the test.

If you have attempted to construct your course of study along the procedure suggested in this book, you should, by this time, be well aware of stating objectives. If the unit method of course construction is being used, some form of evaluation is essential before a student moves on to the next unit in the sequence. The evaluation device might be based upon some well defined behavioral or performance objectives, or upon some other type of criterion measure. In any event, some type of evaluation would seem essential. In some cases, it might lend itself to a type of hands-on performance examination and in others, to a pencil and paper type of examination.

Evaluation Based on Performance Objectives

In a course of study using units and perform-ance objectives, one unit logically leads to the next unit. Unit one should be essential to unit two, and unit two to unit three, and so on. Such units based on performance objectives should be very helpful to shop and lab-oratory instructors. The evaluation aspect is built into each of the stated objectives in well written performance objectives. At times, it will still be desirable to construct an objective or essay type of test to supplement the other forms of evaluation. Such measures should still be consistent with the stated instructional objectives.

If a total of three hundred performance objectives are listed for the course you are teaching, some students might complete all of them. Some level to identify satisfactory performance would have to be estab-lished to identify average or below average performance on the three hundred objectives. However this is a matter of evaluation rather than test construction.

When the performance objectives are written, consideration must be given as to how the criterion measure of the objective will be evaluated. The details of this evaluation must now take place in the test construc-tion phase. For example,

OBJECTIVE   The student, given five resistors and a (VTVM)
#15   vacuum tube voltmeter will be able to measure
               and record the resistance of each, within a toler-
               ance of ±5 percent in five minutes.

To evaluate the student's performance on the objective, some pro-cedure is called for. An accurate reading of the five resistors is essential. An accurate VTVM is necessary. Someone to keep time with an accurate clock or watch is also essential. Some method of recording the informa-tion is also needed, as shown in Figure 14–1.

As indicated earlier, when writing the various objectives, you should have some idea as to how you will evaluate the criterion measure. The example shown in Figure 14–1 is used for Performance Objective #15. It will probably be necessary to have some method of recording the eval-uation of each objective that is a part of your course of study. This re-cording method should be useful to the student being evaluated and to the teacher responsible for the evaluation. A student not meeting the cri-

PERFORMANCE OBJECTIVE #15

Name _____

Time   start _____ stop _____ Total _____

Resistor	Actual Valve	Reading	% Variation
#1	_____	_____	_____
#2	_____	_____	_____
#3	_____	_____	_____
#4	_____	_____	_____
#5	_____	_____	_____

Student ${}^{passed}_{failed}$ the criterion evaluation of Performance Objective #15.

Signed _____

FIGURE 14–1

Recording Evaluation for a Performance Objective

terion measure of performance should know why he failed to do so. After additional experience, he again should be given the opportunity to retake the performance test.

Making Out a Test

The teacher and students must clearly understand the purpose of any test. Are you attempting to measure how well your students have mastered a certain unit of study? Are you attempting to rank your students to determine their individual strengths and weaknesses? Make sure that your students know why they are being tested.

Make an outline or plan for the test you plan to give. Is the plan consistent with the purpose of the test? This plan should be an outline for the test and indicate such things as:

1. Purpose (objective) of the test
2. Time for administration
3. Material to be included, consistent with the purposes
4. Types of questions (performance, objective, essay)
5. Number of questions
6. Method of evaluation
7. Student review or feedback

Many teachers find it helpful to write or type their questions on three by five inch cards. The questions then can form a bank of questions for future use. Poor questions can be so noted or destroyed and replaced with new questions. After teaching the same course or subject a number of times, you will have developed a good number of test questions in your bank. You can then simply pull the number, type, and kind of question you need and give them to your typist for final typing.

Objective questions usually require a single word or number for an answer on a space provided near the question. Good objective tests can do a better testing job in less time than essay tests for many lessons or courses. As a rule, the objective test has more questions and requires a longer preparation time than the essay test.

TYPES OF TEST ITEMS

The following examples show some of the types of questions that can be used in making out a test.

True-False.   In the most common form, the pupil makes a decision as to the most correct answer and writes *true* or *false* in the space provided. Test directions might read as follows:

> Read each statement carefully. Decide whether it is true or false. Print the word true or false in the column at the left before each statement.
>
> ——————————1.   Current is measured by means of a voltmeter.
> ——————————2.   There are 5280 feet in a mile.

Writing test questions takes time. In the true-false questions, by chance alone, a student could score 50 percent. Avoid such words as "never," "always," "all," and "no" in writing true-false type questions. A wise student can often guess correctly that a statement using one of these words is false.

Multiple choice.   The multiple choice type test consists of an incomplete statement or question with several possible answers or completions listed below the question. The multiple choice question measures knowledge more accurately than the true-false question since guessing is reduced. The student marks or write his choice of the one correct answer from the four or five that are given. Test directions might read as follows:

> From each group of possible answers, choose the one you consider best for the statement. Place the letter that identifies the correct answer on the line before each question.
>
> _____3. The octane rating of gasoline tells us about its:
>   a. color
>   b. cost
>   c. purity
>   d. volatility
>   e. anti-knock
>
> _____4. Three 10-ohm resistors are connected in parallel. What is their total resistance?
>   a. 10 ohms
>   b. 3⅓ ohms
>   c. 30 ohms
>   d. 5½ ohms
>   e. 15 ohms

You should avoid including responses that are obviously wrong. Avoid establishing a pattern of correct answers being associated with certain letters. Ending the lead statement with _a_ or _an_ is to be avoided since the correct answer can sometimes be indicated by such words. Asking another faculty member to review your test questions may help you to improve your item writing ability.

Completion or Fill-In.   The student is required to write a word or number which completes the sense of the statement. This type of question is a recall type item. Use this type of item only when it is essential to your needs and consistent with your testing objectives. Test directions for completion type questions might read as follows:

> In the blank of each sentence write the word or number which best completes the sentence.
> 5. The ignition is part of the _____ system of an automobile.
> 6. The smallest division on a micrometer is _____ of an inch.

The length of the line in the sentence should be consistent in each item so as not to give any indication as to the length of the missing word. It is easy, too easy, to copy sentences out of the text books and remove one word and use them as test items. Perhaps such a procedure is suitable if one of your stated instructional objectives is to memorize the contents of a text book. Use caution in following such a practice.

Matching. A matching test has two lists. The student is required to check or mark the items on one list which are best related to the items in the other list. Only a code number or letter needs to be written. The two lists should have unequal numbers of items, but each item should have only one correct answer. Illustrations, charts, or photos can also be used and matched with statements which identify various features. Test directions for matching test items might read as follows:

Place the letter from the list at the right in the proper space at the left to show which word best fits the statement.

( )	1.	Volt	A.	The unit of electrical power
( )	2.	Ampere	B.	The unit of electrical force
( )	3.	Ohm		pressure
( )	4.	Watt	C.	The unit of electrical resistance
( )	5.	Coulomb	D.	The unit of current

It takes times to contruct good matching test items. The basic question remains as to whether the matching type test is the best type of test for the information you are attempting to sample.

Essay. Essay type questions require the student to express himself in his own words. Such questions when evaluated are done so more on a subjective basis than on an objective basis.

An objective type test can usually cover a broad field of information in a given period of time. Essay questions take more time and usually cover only a limited field of knowledge. Essay questions are relatively easy to prepare but very time consuming to score.

Essay questions should encourage pupils to organize their own ideas and express them clearly. If this is one of the stated objectives, you should find essay questions to be of value to you and your students.

Performance. Performance test items require the student to use both his mind and hands in the solution to a problem. Performance test items are comparable to the criterion measures specified in well written behavioral or performance objectives.

This type of test is the most valuable tool for the shop and laboratory teacher in evaluating the performance of his students. The teacher is able to observe and measure the individual's procedural techniques and the quality of the final product.

A well constructed performance test will usually include directions for the person who will administer the test, directions for the student, a drawing or description of the job, a time limit, and a check list for evaluating the various phases of the job.

Performance testing is a very time consuming project for the teacher but of real value to both student and teacher. Performance tests are the best evaluation devices a shop or laboratory teacher can use to measure individual student achievement in terms of the stated course objectives.

Take Home Examination.   You may find take home examinations to be of value in your teaching situation. A take home examination is as its name implies, an examination that the student takes with him and completes on his own time. If the nature of the test items are such as to require research on the part of the student, a take home examination may be the answer. It is expected that on such examinations, the students use whatever resources are available to them.

The success or failure of such an examination will depend to a large extent on the students in your class and how you prepared them for the evaluation. Do not let take home examinations be the main type of your evaluation procedures. Use them only when their use is consistent with the stated course objectives.

A modified form of the take home examination is the open book examination. This type of examination is conducted in the school and encourages the student to use reference materials and text books in completing the examination. Since it is an in-school examination, some specified amount of time is usually given to the students to complete it.

ANSWER SHEETS

You may find the use of an answer sheet to be helpful on objective type examinations. Rather than have the students write the answers to the questions on the examination, a separate answer sheet is provided for the students to record their answers on.

The use of answer sheets for objective type tests usually makes the correction procedure much easier for the teacher. The answers to fifty or more questions can usually be put on one side of a standard size piece of paper. Such a procedure eliminates going through five or ten pages of the normal examination.

The students should be allowed and encouraged to first place the answers on the question sheet. After they have answered all the questions, the final answers are placed on the answer sheet. The directions must state that the only answers to be considered will be those on the answer sheet.

Another advantage of using answer sheets is that the student may be permitted to keep the question part of the examination and hand in just the answer sheet. The teacher, time permitting, could immediately begin to review the items on the examination. Since the students have the answers on the question sheet, they would have immediate feedback as to how they did on the examination. If time did not permit an in-class review, the students could take the questions and correct them on their own time.

Commercially prepared answer sheets are also available from a number of suppliers. Some are self-scoring. The student erases a block-out material that exposes a symbol that indicates if his choice was the correct answer. If his choice on a four choice multiple choice type item was not correct, he goes on to make a second or even a third choice until he gets the correct answer.

Return and Explanation of Tests

If an examination is important enough to construct and administer, it seems essential that it be promptly corrected and returned to the students. Students are usually very interested in how well they did on the examination, and every effort should be made to review the results with them as soon as possible.

The correct answer for each item should be reviewed so that students will know where they went wrong. Part of the value of any examination should be its value as a learning device. This should take place in the review of the test items.

The students should be encouraged to keep all returned papers, including examinations, for future reference and study.

Take time to review how the grades assigned to the students as a result of an examination fit into the total evaluation procedure. Explain the evaluation procedure used on the examination. It is easy to indicate the various raw scores, median, and mean score of the test. Each student will know his own score and be able to determine how well he scored on the examination in relation to the other students in the class. This does not imply that the student who had the lowest score did not work to the best of his ability. All that is implied is a ranking of the test scores on one examination. The ability of each student must be considered in the final evaluation procedure.

DISCUSSION QUESTIONS

1. Divide the members of the class into a number of small groups. Each group should react to the following question: List the advantages and disadvantages of performance objectives in the testing procedure.

2. By means of a class discussion, consider the following question: What are the advantages of the objective type question in the testing procedure used in shop and laboratory teaching? Indicate the disadvantages.

3. By means of a class discussion, consider the following questions:
   a)   Why should we test?
   b)   When should we test?
   c)   How should we test?

ASSIGNMENTS

1. Prepare a forty-item test for your specialization. The test should consist of ten of each of the following:
   a)   True-false items
   b)   Multiple choice items
   c)   Completion items
   d)   Matching items

2. Write five performance objectives for students in your class. Develop an evaluation recording technique for each performance objective. (Use Figure 14–1 as an example.)

3. Specify your test construction criteria.

ADDITIONAL REFERENCES

Adult Vocational-Industrial Teacher's Guide. Albany: The University of the State of New York, The State Education Department, 1956.

Armstrong, Robert, *et al. The Development and Evaluation of Behavioral Objectives.* Worthington, Ohio: Charles A. Jones Publishing Company, 1970.

Green, John, *Teacher Made Tests.* New York: Harper & Row, Publishers, 1963.

Katz, Martin, ed., *Making the Classroom Test: A Guide for Teachers.* Princeton: Educational Testing Service, 1961.

Chapter 15 EVALUATION AND GRADING

The Purpose of Evaluation

The purpose of evaluation is to assess the degree of success that the learner had in mastering certain performance or instructional material that was presented to him. The person conducting or assessing the evaluation should keep in mind the individual differences and the abilities of the learners.

The practical side of evaluation, that each teacher must realize, in most school systems is to determine if a student passes or fails a course. Clearly stated objectives or criteria understood by the students will help make such evaluations easier.

As time goes on perhaps schools will move closer to the self-pacing concept of instruction making the educational system a zero-reject system. The educational system should be geared to success, not failure. Your efforts to use the self-pacing system and performance objectives might be a step in the right direction.

The Purpose of Grades

The grades assigned to students on tests or for final evaluation usually indicate some degree of success or failure on the test or term work. The method or system used for grading in the school must be followed by all teachers.

The grade given is the result of some evaluation technique used by the teacher. All the students must understand this technique if the grade is to be of any value to them.

If a student received a 66 as his final grade in automotive mechanics, what does this really mean? If 65 is the minimum passing average, it means he passed the course. If 70 is the minimum passing average, it means he failed the course by 4. If a 66 is passing, does it mean the student mastered 66 percent of the course work? Does it mean he is 66 percent of an automotive mechanic? Does it mean he can do 66 percent of the work normally expected of an automotive mechanic? Only the person responsible for the evaluation can answer these questions. The evaluator must also be able to explain the grade to a potential employer of the student.

Individual Differences

In arriving at a final evaluation for a class and, in turn, each student, always attempt to evaluate each individual in terms of his own abilities. The decision that you as the teacher must make concerning each student can have a positive or negative effect upon the student.

Each student has his own strengths and weaknesses, and evaluation in a course should take these into consideration. You can, and will, find extreme situations. The high ability student who, for any number of reasons, fails to perform to the level of his ability versus the low ability student who over-performs. In such situations, the teacher is truly a decision-maker, and he alone must stand accountable for the decision.

Statistics for Teachers

This section reviews some of the most common statistical terms with which a teacher should be familiar. It is designed as an aid for shop and laboratory teachers in the grading and evaluation of students.

Item. An item is a single question or exercise in a test.

Item Weight. Item weight is the raw score point value of the item. You should show the credit for each item on a test. This should tell the student which questions are of most value and those of lesser value.

Item Analysis. Item analyis is a basic operation that all published tests go through. It is seldom applied to teacher-made tests. It can be of value to the maker of a teacher made test and can be easily done. The analysis simply tells the teacher how many students had each item correct or incorrect. The information can be easily obtained by asking the class how many students had item #1, #2, etc., incorrect and recording the tally. The tally should indicate what information is and is not clearly understood by the students.

Raw Scores. This is the first quantitative result obtained in scoring a test, usually the number of right answers.

Range. The range consists of the difference between the lowest and highest scores obtained on a test by some group.

Mean. It is the sum of a set of scores divided by the number of scores. This can, and often is, also described as the arithmetic mean or the average.

Median. This is the middle score in a distribution of scores. The point that divides the group into two equal parts. Half of the group scores below the median and half above it.

Mode. This is the score or value that occurs most frequently in a distribution.

N. It is the symbol commonly used to represent the number of cases in a distribution.

After a test is given, some evaluation of the results should occur. If the raw scores are listed with the highest score first and the lowest last, it is very easy to determine the range, mean, and median. This gives each student a clear idea of how well he did on the test compared to the others in the class. This procedure does not take into account the individual differences existing among the members of the class.

DISCUSSION QUESTIONS

1. Divide the class into a number of small groups. Ask each group the following question: How do you account for the individual differences of the students in your class when making final evaluations?

2. Discuss various ways shop teachers can evaluate student performance on performance objectives. How can such performance be reported to students, parents, and employers?

3. Review some practical examples involving the following:
   a) Determine the mean score from a set of scores.
   b) Determine the median score from a set of scores.
   c) Review item analysis procedure.

ASSIGNMENTS

1. Perform an item analysis on the next test you administer. Submit a tally sheet of the result of the analysis. Comment on the item analysis results.

2. Using the same test as in Item #1, determine the range, mean, and median of the set of scores obtained on the test.

3. Define standard deviation and determine the standard deviates of the test administered in Item #1.

ADDITIONAL REFERENCES

Katz, Martin, ed., *Short Cut Statistics for Teacher Made Tests.* Princeton: Educational Testing Service, 1964.

Ross, C.C. and Julian C. Stanley, *Measurement in Today's Schools.* New York: Prentice-Hall, Inc., 1954.

VanDalen, Deobold B., *Understanding Educational Research.* New York: McGraw-Hill Book Company, 1962.

INDEX